CONSUMERISM
New Challenges For Marketing

Edited by:
Norman Kangun
University of Houston

Lee Richardson
Louisiana State University

790671

AMERICAN
MARKETING
ASSOCIATION

222 S. Riverside Plaza • Chicago, Illinois 60606 • (312) 648-0536

Cover Design by Mary Jo Galluppi

Library of Congress Cataloging in Publication Data

Conference on Consumerism, Baton Rouge, La., 1976.
    Consumerism : new challenges for marketing.

    Includes index.
    1. Consumer protection--United States--Congresses.
2. Marketing--Social aspects--United States--Congresses.
I. Kangun, Norman.   II. Richardson, Lee, 1940-
III. American Marketing Association.   IV. Title.
HC110.C63C594 1976   381'.3   77-7370
ISBN 0-87757-097-3

CONTENTS

PREFACE

One of the most important phenomena of the last fifteen years has been the growth of consumerism—a movement designed to assert and to enhance the consumer's voice in activities that affect him. Concurrently, the consumerism movement has been joined by government representatives at all levels who have become increasingly skeptical of certain business practices. It seems inevitable that business, exposed to consumerism pressures, will have to actively demonstrate that it is truly sensitive to consumer desires. Similarly, the goals, purposes, and directions that the consumerism movement takes will change in response to dynamic and evolving social forces.

The American Marketing Association historically has attempted to meet the need for information about macro issues relating to marketing by publishing reports of conferences. This book focuses on consumerism and the challenges it poses for marketing and public policymakers. It is a compilation of selected papers presented at the American Marketing Association's conference on consumerism which was held at Louisiana State University in March 1976.

While a successful conference is the result of the efforts of many people, a special debt of gratitude is owed to Keith K. Cox, then AMA Vice-President for Marketing Education, for encouraging us to hold this conference. Similarly, the Marketing Department of the College of Business Administration at Louisiana State University is to be thanked for hosting the conference. Finally, Becky Sepolio and Suzanne Bryan at the University of Houston are to be commended for their efforts in typing parts of this book.

Norman Kangun
University of Houston

Lee Richardson
Louisiana State University

v

PART 1

Consumer Regulation: Some Directions for Research

AN EXPLORATORY INVESTIGATION OF SELECTED ASPECTS OF THE MAGNUSON-MOSS WARRANTY ACT

Norman Kangun and Keith K. Cox
The University of Houston

William A. Staples
Drake University

This paper examines consumer feelings about product warranties. It focuses specifically on an evaluation of consumer perceptions of certain provisions of the Magnuson-Moss Warranty Act.

In recent years, consumerists have increasingly questioned the effectiveness of many product warranties in protecting the consumer. According to one writer, warranty complaints were among the most numerous and passionate of those received by Consumers Union [3]. A 1973 survey of 106 warranties by the Major Appliance Consumer Action Panel (industry sponsored) turned up serious shortcomings in a great many warranties. Among the more common were: (1) failure to mention specific parts covered by the warranty, (2) failure to set forth the duration of the warranty coverage, and (3) presentation of the coverage terms in confusing legal language [6]. Further, a House subcommittee examined warranties from 51 major U.S. companies and found that the vast majority of them helped the sellers dodge their legal obligations by using either disclaimers or ambiguous phrases [1]. Despite the expressed concern with product warranties, research in this area is still limited [3, 4, 5, 7].

The study discussed in this paper addresses the following questions relating to product warranties: (1) How important are product warranties to consumers relative to price, style, manufacturer's reputation, and other factors in a durable goods purchase situation? (2) Do consumers assign greater value to warranties that are clearly

3

written and easy to understand? (3) Does specifically designating the warranty as either "full" or "limited," which is mandatory under the new Magnuson-Moss Warranty Act, assist consumers in recognizing value in different types of warranties? and (4) How much are consumers willing to pay for warranties offering greater protection, particularly those meeting the minimum standards required by law for designation as a "full" warranty?

First, we will explore some of the basic provisions of the Magnuson-Moss Warranty Act. Then, we will analyze the methodology and findings of this study. We will conclude by examining the managerial implications of product warranties for the future.

THE MAGNUSON-MOSS WARRANTY ACT: A BRIEF REVIEW

Responding to considerable consumer pressure, Congress passed the Magnuson-Moss Warranty Act in January 1975 [2]. The legislative aims of the act were to provide minimum disclosure standards, and minimum federal content standards, for written consumer product warranties. More pragmatically, the act seeks to: (1) improve the accuracy of information available to consumers in written warranties, (2) prevent deception, (3) stimulate competition in marketing consumer products, and (4) encourage warrantors to establish procedures whereby consumer disputes can be fairly and quickly settled through informal dispute settlement mechanisms.

The new law, which went into effect on July 4, 1975, is administered by the Federal Trade Commission. Under the law, written warranties must meet certain conditions. The product must be free of defects and perform satisfactorily for a reasonable period of time, and the seller must take appropriate action if the product fails during its normal life. The act encourages manufacturers to write warranties that are simple and easy to understand, and it applies to consumer products distributed in commerce and normally used for personal, family, or household purposes.

Among the more important provisions in the new warranty law is the one that establishes standards that distinguish between a "full" and a "limited" warranty. To qualify for a "full" warranty designa-

4

tion, the warrantor must satisfy the following federal minimum standards:

1. A defect in a consumer product must be remedied within a reasonable time and without charge.
2. No limits can be placed on implied warranties.
3. Any exclusion or limitation of consequential damages must appear clearly and conspicuously on the face of the warranty.
4. If the defect or malfunction is not remedied after a reasonable number of attempts by the warrantor, the warrantor must permit the consumer to elect either refund or replacement without charge for the product or part.
5. The warrantor may not require the consumer to do anything as a condition to obtain compliance with the warranty other than give notice of the defect or malfunction unless the warrantor can show that the condition required to obtain compliance with the warranty is reasonable.

Conversely, a warranty that does not meet these standards is automatically designated a "limited" warranty.

METHODOLOGY

A convenience sample of 149 consumers were interviewed in a large shopping center in Houston in fall 1975. Each subject was asked, first, a series of general questions about warranties, and then specific questions about warranties when purchasing a refrigerator. The respondents were randomly assigned to groups and given one of four different written warranties to evaluate. The four different warranty treatments, in a two-by-two factorial design, were:

Warranty Designation

		Labeled	Unlabeled
Extent	*Full*	L–F	U–F
of			
Coverage	*Limited*	L–L	U–L

5

Given the nature of the sample, the results should not be considered representative of durable goods purchases. They do, however, provide tentative clues regarding consumer reaction to certain warranty changes mandated by law. Further, the results of this study may have considerable external validity. First, consumers were used rather than students; second, the interviews were collected in a shopping center—a realistic purchasing environment.

FINDINGS

Importance of Warranties

To learn the importance that consumers attach to product warranties in general, subjects were asked to evaluate eight factors that could influence their decision to buy a refrigerator (Table 1). Approximately 90 percent rated manufacturer warranties as either extremely or very important. This rating was higher than any of the other factors, including manufacturer's reputation, storage capacity, and price. The manufacturer's warranty appears to be of major interest to consumers in the purchase of a refrigerator.

TABLE 1

CONSUMER IMPORTANCE RATINGS OF
REFRIGERATOR PURCHASE FACTORS

Factor	% of Respondents Answering Extremely or Very Important[a]
Storage capacity	77.2
Manufacturer's reputation	81.2
Total price	75.8
Credit terms	51.0
Store purchased from	62.4
Warranty by manufacturer	89.9
Style/design/features	62.3
Color	36.9

[a] N = 149.

Value of Warranties

Subjects also were asked to judge the value added to the product by a specific refrigerator warranty. Four different warranties were randomly assigned to the respondents. As noted above, the warranties differed in two respects: (1) extent of coverage—limited or full; and (2) label designation—present or absent. More specifically, with respect to warranty coverage, the limited warranties differed from the full warranties in the following ways:

1. Implied warranties were excluded.
2. The cost of labor was to be paid by the purchaser.
3. The warranty covered only the original purchaser.
4. The warranty excluded consequential damages.
5. The registration card had to be returned to the manufacturer for the warranty to be operative.
6. Proof of misuse was to be determined by the manufacturer.

With respect to label designation, some warranties were labeled and others were not. The Magnuson-Moss Act requires that all written warranties be labeled as either full or limited to minimize consumer confusion. The dependent variable in this case was the respondent's judgment regarding the degree of value added to the product by the warranties.

The results indicate that respondents perceived full warranties as adding greater value to the product than limited warranties (Table 2). This strong difference occurred whether the warranty was labeled or unlabeled. In fact, labeling the warranties had little effect on the respondents' rating of the value added to the product.

Amount Willing to Pay

In an open-ended question, all subjects were asked how much they would be willing to pay for a warranty when considering the purchase of a $400 refrigerator (Table 3). Respondents who were shown the full warranty were willing to spend significantly more money for that warranty than the respondents who were shown the limited warranty. Almost 60 percent of the respondents shown the full warranty were willing to pay at least $30 or more for this war-

TABLE 2

PROPORTION OF RESPONDENTS WHO SAID WARRANTY ADDS SOME OR GREAT VALUE

Warranty Designation	Extent of Coverage	
	Full	Limited
Labeled	92.5% (40)[a]	61.8% (34)
Unlabeled	94.7% (38)	59.5% (37)

[a] Number in parentheses indicates cell size.

ranty, while less than one-fourth of the respondents shown the limited warranty were willing to spend that amount.

IMPLICATIONS AND CONCLUSIONS

This study focused on consumers' feelings about product warranties for a refrigerator and, to a larger extent, whether consumers perceive certain provisions of the Magnuson-Moss Warranty Act favorably. Respondents from our sample generally believed product warranties to be an important factor in durable goods purchase situations. They saw full warranties as adding more value to the product than limited warranties, regardless of whether the warranty was labeled. They also tended to be willing to pay more for a full warranty than a limited one.

The finding that consumers attach as much or more importance to a product warranty as they do to factors such as price, manufacturer's reputation, and style in the purchase of a refrigerator is not surprising. For products purchased infrequently, perceived by consumers as complex, and requiring substantial outlays of money, the product warranty is likely to be judged highly important.

8

TABLE 3
AMOUNT RESPONDENTS WILLING TO PAY FOR THE TWO TYPES OF WARRANTIES

Amount Willing to Pay	Limited Warranty (n = 67)	Full Warranty (n = 72)
Nothing	38.8%	11.1%
$1-$29	37.3%	30.6%
$30 and over	23.9%	58.3%
	100.0%	100.0%

$\chi^2 = 21.29$, significant at .01 level.

The unfavorable publicity given to warranty deficiencies, particularly in the consumer durable category, also may explain why consumers attach more importance to product warranties. For example, the President's Task Force Report on Appliance warranties concluded in 1969:

> The majority of the major appliance warranties currently in use contain exemptions and exclusions which are unfair to the purchaser and which are unnecessary from the standpoint of protecting the manufacturer from unjustified claims or excessive liability. [6]

Many durable goods manufacturers have used the warranty to limit their liability, not as a marketing tool to attract customers. Our data suggest that there is a sizable group of consumers with considerable interest in warranty coverage. Failure of marketers to devote more attention and resources to providing better warranties may result in lost sales.

As noted earlier, the act requires that the terms and conditions of written warranties be fully and conspicuously disclosed in simple and readily understood language. To be designated "full," as opposed to "limited," a warranty must meet minimum federal standards. When our subjects were given simple and easily understood full and limited

9

warranties to evaluate, a significantly greater proportion of those exposed to the full warranty perceived it as having some or a great deal of value than did those exposed to the limited warranty. When consumers are given warranties written in simple language, label designations appear to be superfluous in judging the value of the warranty. From the standpoint of both public policy and marketplace effectiveness, simplified warranty language may convey more relevant information to consumers than warranty labels.

Finally, most respondents appeared to be aware that good warranties cost money. The overwhelming majority were willing (within limits) to pay for better warranty protection. Full warranties that meet minimum standards prescribed by law do add value to the product in the eyes of consumers. As such, more comprehensive warranties appear to have great potential as a competitive promotional tool. In fact, Whirlpool strengthened its competitive market position with the development and promotion of their warranties.

To summarize, the research findings reported here suggest the following conclusions:

1. Most respondents considered warranties, moreso than other factors, as either extremely or very important in the purchase of refrigerators.
2. When the warranties were written clearly and simply, most respondents could recognize the value of full warranties even in the absence of an explicit label designation.
3. The majority of respondents were willing to pay more for better warranty coverage, thus offering manufacturers another means of product differentiation.

This research study is not without its limitations. The findings must be viewed as tentative because of: (1) the small sample, (2) the judgmental nature of the sampling procedure, (3) the fact that our subjects were responding to a hypothetical situation rather than a real purchase situation, and (4) our focus was on one consumer durable product only.

At this time, it is too early to measure the full impact of the Warranty Act on consumer and manufacturer behavior. Future questions marketers must address include:

1. How have consumers responded to the Warranty Act; that is, has the law diminished disenchantment with warranties?
2. How have companies responded to the act? Have they altered their warranties? If so, in which direction?
3. To the extent that some companies have chosen to provide consumers with full warranties, have the companies benefited in the marketplace through increased sales and higher profits?

REFERENCES

1. *Consumer Product Warranties,* Staff Report of the Subcommittee on Commerce and Finance of the House Interstate and Foreign Commerce Committee, Sept. 17, 1974.

2. 15 USC 2301.

3. Fisk, George. "Guidelines for Warranty Service After Sale," *Journal of Marketing,* 34 (Jan. 1970), 63-7.

4. Kendall, C. L. and Frederick A. Russ. "Warranty and Complaint Policies: An Opportunity for Marketing Management," *Journal of Marketing,* 39 (Apr. 1975), 36-43.

5. Lehmann, Donald R. and Lyman E. Ostlund. "Consumer Perceptions of Product Warranties: An Exploratory Study," in Scott Ward and Peter Wright, eds., *Advances in Consumer Research.* Atlanta, Association for Consumer Research, 1973.

6. "Product Warranties: Congress Lends a Helping Hand," *Consumer Reports,* 40 (Mar. 1975), 164-5.

7. Udell, Jon G. and Evan E. Anderson. "The Product Warranty as an Element of Competitive Strategy," *Journal of Marketing,* 32, (Oct. 1968), 1-8.

THE TRUTH-IN-LIFE-INSURANCE MOVEMENT*

Joseph M. Belth
Indiana University

The author discusses the background of the life insurance disclosure movement and describes some of the deceptive sales practices used in the life insurance business. He then offers a system of information disclosure that would provide adequate information to prospective life insurance buyers and present policyholders.

Individual life insurance buyers and policyholders usually do not receive accurate, reliable, timely, incisive information about their life insurance. For this reason and because of the strength of the consumer movement generally, efforts to enact "truth-in-life-insurance" legislation are gaining momentum. This paper discusses the background of the life insurance disclosure movement, describes some of the deceptive sales practices used in the life insurance industry, and illustrates a disclosure system that would provide adequate information to life insurance buyers and policyholders.

BACKGROUND

The problems of price measurement in life insurance have been discussed for many years among persons within or close to the industry [9]. In 1966, a "rigorous system of price disclosure" was suggested for the life insurance industry [4]. But it was not until September 1967 that the subject gained widespread public attention as the result of a front-page story in the *Wall Street Journal* [27].

---

*This paper was prepared in March 1976 and was not updated prior to publication.

12

In March 1968 in a speech delivered in Hartford, I made the following statement:

I would like to mention what might be considered a classic example of the need for price disclosure in life insurance. The federal government, through the Veterans Administration, made a limited amount of low-priced life insurance available to veterans of World War I, World War II and the Korean War. In 1965 a program known as Servicemen's Group Life Insurance was established on a cooperative basis with the life insurance industry. The serviceman is provided with a limited amount of low-priced coverage, and the veteran has the privilege of converting it without evidence of insurability within 120 days following discharge. To exercise the conversion privilege, the veteran buys a regular policy from any one of a substantial number of companies operating in his state of domicile. For example, if a currently discharged Indiana veteran inquires about his conversion privilege, he is furnished with an alphabetical list of 278 companies—and no price guidance. A rigorous system of price disclosure would provide the kind of information the veteran needs in order to avoid paying an unnecessarily high price for his life insurance protection.

The above statement was brought to the attention of U.S. Senator Philip A. Hart, chairman of the Subcommittee on Antitrust and Monopoly of the Committee on the Judiciary, who thereupon engaged in an important exchange of correspondence with William J. Driver, then administrator of veterans affairs. Senator Hart urged the Veterans Administration to compile life insurance price information and supply such information to Vietnam veterans. Mr. Driver declined to do so.

In October 1968 in a speech before a life insurance industry group, Senator Hart referred to the possibility of truth-in-life-insurance legislation. He made the following statements:

Obviously if it makes sense to tell consumers how much of what is in a package on a supermarket shelf or how much interest they will pay for using someone else's money, it makes sense to tell them how much they are paying for death protec-

13

tion and how much they are saving when they plunk down a life insurance premium.

Hopefully your industry will think so too—and start supplying the information.

If not—watch for Truth in Life Insurance to follow Truth in Packaging and Truth in Lending through the legislative mill.

Because that's the way people are thinking in consumerland. [20]

In November 1968 similar comments were made by Wilbur J. Cohen, then secretary of Health, Education, and Welfare, in testimony at a Federal Trade Commission hearing. Secretary Cohen suggested the need for "more uniformity, more comprehensive protection, and more price comparison" in various areas of insurance, including life insurance [10].

In March 1969 as a direct result of Senator Hart's admonition and Secretary Cohen's comment, three life insurance trade associations appointed a prestigious industry committee to examine the price disclosure problem. The committee's report was released in May 1970 [26]. While the report contained suggestions that, if implemented, would represent a major forward step, several crucial areas were left untouched.

The committee's major recommendation was that the interest-adjusted method be used in making cost comparisons among similar policies issued by different companies. This method, as its name implies, takes interest into account in evaluating the premiums that the policyholder pays to the insurance company and in evaluating the payments made to the policyholder by the insurance company. It differs from the traditional net cost method which involves the simple addition of amounts payable at different times. The latter method, widely used in the life insurance industry, understates the price of life insurance and distorts comparisons even between similar policies.

The committee's report did not discuss the question of yearly price information at the point of sale nor of periodic information after the sale. Furthermore, the report failed to deal with a key aspect of Senator Hart's admonition—the need to inform the buyer about the extent to which he is buying protection and the extent to which he is putting away savings when he buys a cash-value life insurance policy.

The three trade associations that created the committee "received" the report and authorized its publication. They did not approve or endorse the report, however, apparently fearful of violating the antitrust laws [21]. A major insurance industry trade publisher developed a comprehensive volume of price information based on the interest-adjusted method recommended by the committee [8]. A few companies placed interest-adjusted cost figures in the rate books they furnish to their agents. But the life insurance industry's primary reaction to the committee report was silence.

In September 1971 Virginia H. Knauer, the president's special assistant for consumer affairs, urged the life insurance industry to do something about the report of its own committee [25]. Mrs. Knauer had been prodded by Joe A. Mintz, a Texas insurance agent and consumer advocate. As a result, many additional companies placed interest-adjusted cost figures in their rate books.

In April 1972 the Pennsylvania insurance department issued a *Shopper's Guide to Life Insurance* which showed interest-adjusted price figures for numerous major companies operating in Pennsylvania [28]. The guide was made available free to the public and received extensive national publicity [5].

In May 1972 at a consumer symposium held at the University of Wisconsin, I recommended an information disclosure system for life insurance buyers and policyholders [24]. The recommended system was similar but not identical to the system described later in this paper.

In August 1972 the Wisconsin insurance department promulgated an administrative rule requiring life insurance companies operating in Wisconsin to make interest-adjusted price figures available to buyers at or prior to delivery of the policy [29]. The rule took effect January 1, 1973.

In February 1973 Senator Hart conducted four days of hearings on life insurance. The hearings were designed to explore the need for life insurance disclosure legislation [12, 13, 14, 22].

15

In April 1973 the American Life Insurance Association—a major trade association that grew out of a merger between the American Life Convention and the Life Insurance Association of America, two of the three associations that had created the aforementioned industry committee in 1969—announced its support of the interest-adjusted method. The announcement was made at a hearing conducted by Insurance Commissioner John H. Durkin of New Hampshire on a proposed regulation that would have imposed far more rigorous disclosure requirements on the life insurance industry.[1] Apparently the combined pressure from Mrs. Knauer, Senator Hart, and Commissioner Durkin at long last had prompted the industry to endorse the report that three years earlier had been merely "received" [11].

In June 1973 the National Association of Insurance Commissioners adopted a model regulation based on the interest-adjusted method. The regulation was adopted on an interim basis pending the results of a series of research projects that were being conducted by various industry groups and by Senator Hart's subcommittee staff [16]. In the months that followed several states adopted disclosure regulations similar to the NAIC model. Among these were Arkansas, California, Pennsylvania, Texas and West Virginia.

In March 1974 in his second speech to a life insurance industry group (more than five years after his landmark first speech), Senator Hart dropped the other shoe: He announced that his staff was drafting a truth-in-life-insurance bill [7, 17]. He said the bill would consist of two major parts: (1) a rigorous system of disclosure to life insurance buyers and policyholders, and (2) a section concerning life insurance agents' contracts designed to make agents more independent of their primary companies.

In July 1974 one additional day of hearings was conducted by Senator Hart. At these hearings the results of a massive life insurance

---

[1]Shortly after the hearing, Commissioner Durkin resigned his post, and no disclosure regulation was promulgated. He is now the junior United States Senator from New Hampshire, having won a hotly contested runoff following one of the closest elections in American history.

price study conducted by the subcommittee staff were made public [15, 23].

In July 1975 Senator Hart introduced his proposed truth-in-life-insurance legislation, bill S.2065 entitled "The Consumer Insurance Information and Fairness Act" [19]. As expected, it provided for rigorous disclosure to life insurance buyers at the point of sale as well as rigorous disclosure to policyholders periodically after the sale. It also contained a section dealing with life insurance agents' contracts. The Federal Trade Commission would be charged with the responsibility for administering the provisions of the bill, and it was referred to the Senate Committee on Commerce.[2] At the time of this writing hearings on the bill were tentatively scheduled for June 1976.

DECEPTIVE SALES PRACTICES

The marketing of individual life insurance is characterized by a variety of deceptive sales practices [1]. The word *deceptive* as used here refers to information that tends to give the buyer an erroneous impression of important relationships. The emphasis in this definition is on the buyer, and it is not intended to suggest that the deception is necessarily deliberate on the part of the life insurance agent. Indeed, many agents probably do not realize they are engaging in deceptive sales practices.

Class A Practices

Deceptive life insurance practices may be divided into three categories. Class A practices apply to a single policy year and involve a misallocation of the interest factor. Consider an analogy. Suppose a person deposits $1,000 each year into a savings account and that

---

[2]Senator Hart had indicated that he planned to retire from the Senate when his current term expires at the end of 1976. His life insurance bill may not be left without a champion, however, because Senator Durkin (the former New Hampshire insurance commissioner referred to earlier) is a member of the Commerce Committee.

the account is credited with $629 of interest in the tenth year. If it is suggested that all of the $629 arose from the tenth year's deposit of $1,000, the implication would be that the depositor earned 62.9 percent interest on that deposit. If the interest were allocated properly, however, most of it would be allocated to earlier deposits and the correct interest rate would be 5 percent.

From the buyer's viewpoint a cash-value life insurance policy properly may be considered as a package consisting of protection and savings. Under this view, the rate of return on the savings element and the price of the protection element are two sides of the same coin, and the effect of Class A deceptive sales practices is either to overstate the rate of return on the savings element or to understate the price of the protection element.

An example of Class A deception involving an overstatement of the rate of return on the savings element is contained in a 1970 life insurance sales magazine article [18]. In the article the author states that $989 per year is the difference between the premium for $100,000 of nonparticipating decreasing term insurance issued at age 30 by the American General Life Insurance Company and the premium for $100,000 of nonparticipating straight life issued at the same age by the same company. The author of the article attributes the full amount of the cash-value increase in the straight-life policy in any given year to the $989 difference paid in that year. For example, in the tenth year, he shows an "annual increase in assets" of $1,427. He attributes that increase to the $989 difference paid in the tenth year and then shows the "annual percent tax free profit" that year as 44.3 percent. This figure is based on a misallocation of the interest factor. When a reasonable allocation of the interest is carried out (by assuming that the price of the protection is equal to the tenth year cost of the term policy), the figure is 3.8 percent.

Class A practices involving an understatement of the price of the protection element are more widely used than those involving an overstatement of the rate of return on the savings element. Perhaps the most common examples of Class A deception involving understatement of the price of protection are the ledger statements used by many life insurance companies.

18

Consider a ledger statement for a $100,000 participating straight life policy issued to a man aged 40.[3] In the tenth policy year, for example, the entire increase in cash value ($2,100) and the tenth year dividend ($435) are subtracted from the tenth year premium ($2,448). The result is a tenth year cost of *minus* $87. This figure is based on a misallocation of the interest factor. When a reasonable allocation of the interest is carried out (by assuming a five percent rate of return on the savings element of the policy), the tenth year cost is *plus* $880.

Class B Practices

Class B practices apply to a period of years and involve comparisons based on the simple addition of amounts payable at different times. Consider another analogy. Jones retained Smith to do a particular job, with the understanding that upon completion Smith would be paid $1,000 per year for 40 years—a total of $40,000. After the job was completed Smith asked Jones to begin the payments, and Jones said:

> Smith, you've done such a great job that I'm going to pay you ten percent more than we agreed upon. I'm going to pay you $600 per year for 30 years and then $2,600 per year for the final ten years. That's a total of $44,000, which is ten percent more than the $40,000 I originally agreed to pay you.

Jones failed to take interest into account in the description of his proposed modification of the agreement. For example, assuming five percent interest, the present value of the payments under the original agreement is $18,017, while the present value of the payments under the proposed modification is $14,562. Thus, what Jones described as an arrangement providing ten percent more for Smith actually provides about nineteen percent less, assuming five percent interest.

---

[3]The figures and the terminology used in this particular example are taken from a ledger statement used in 1971 by the Acacia Mutual Life Insurance Company. Approximately the same approach is found, however, in the ledger statements disseminated by many other companies.

Some presentations involving Class B deception severely understate the price of life insurance protection in a policy, some severely distort price comparisons between similar policies, and some severely distort price comparisons between dissimilar policies. An example of the latter type of distortion appeared in a talk given at the 1970 annual meeting of the National Association of Life Underwriters [6]. The talk dealt with the advantages of straight life over term insurance. The speaker first indicated that, for a $100,000 participating straight-life policy issued at age 25 and continued to age 65, the "net return over cost" was $30,923. Then he said that, for a $100,000 participating one-year renewable term policy over the same period, the "cost of term insurance" was $34,579. He concluded that the "total difference" in favor of the straight-life policy was $65,502.[4] This analysis is based on the simple addition of dollar amounts payable at different times. When an assumed interest rate of five percent is applied to the situation, the interest-adjusted cost of the straight-life policy, expressed in present-value terms, is $9,163, and the corresponding figure for the term policy is $9,733. These figures still favor the straight-life policy, but by $570 rather than $65,502.

Class C Practices

Class C practices involve presentations that are false, but their falsity usually is difficult to detect because of their complexity. Here is an example of Class C deception. The procedure is designed to persuade a term insurance policyholder to convert to straight life, and the presentation is as follows:

> Mr. Jones, you do have a lot of protection in that term policy for the $300 it costs. You know, of course, that there is no cash value in it. It's the kind of policy you have to die to beat.
>
> Did you know, Mr. Jones, that the permanent kind of life insurance can be so arranged that you eventually get all of your money back if you don't die? [Wait for answer.]
>
> Since you get all of your money back, the cost of permanent

---

[4]The data used in the comparison were for a straight-life policy issued by the New York Life Insurance Company and a term policy issued by the Manufacturers Life Insurance Company.

insurance is really just the interest on your money, isn't it? [Wait for answer.]

Now, here's an intriguing point. Since the term premium pays just for the insurance, with no return, isn't that term premium just like interest on the permanent premium that buys the same amount of insurance? [Wait for answer. Repeat if necessary.]

In that case, you are paying about 30 percent interest, Mr. Jones. Let me show you what I mean. At your age of 30, your $50,000 term policy costs you $300 per year. Whole life, which would return all of your money eventually, would cost you $1,000 per year for the same amount. The term premium is interest on the permanent. That's where I got the 30 percent interest figure. Don't you think that's pretty high? Can you invest money anywhere for that much return? [Wait for answer.]

Well, you can make just such an investment here, by converting that term to permanent life insurance! [30]

The major flaw in this presentation may not be readily apparent. In the first year, the $300 term premium would be thirty percent of the straight-life premium. In the second year, however, even disregarding interest, the $300 term premium would be fifteen percent of the $2,000 total paid into the straight-life policy. Similarly, and again disregarding interest, the figures would be ten percent in the third year, three percent in the tenth year, two percent in the fifteenth year, and so forth.

A DISCLOSURE SYSTEM

To develop an effective system of life insurance information disclosure knowledgeable observers must agree on precisely what information should be included in the disclosure system and how that information should be displayed. *Information* in this context refers to both benefit information and price information. In this section, I will explain and illustrate a disclosure system I have recommended [2].

Broadly speaking two forms of disclosure are necessary. First, there must be disclosure to the buyer at the point of sale. Second, there must be periodic, continuing disclosure to the policyholder—preferably once a year.

Point-of-Sale Disclosure

Certain information should be disclosed to the life insurance buyer at or prior to delivery of the policy. The phrase *at or prior to delivery* is important. The necessary disclosure is sufficiently elaborate that it would have to be prepared at the home office of the insurance company. If the disclosure statement were not requested in advance, the logical procedure would be for the statement to be prepared at the same time the policy is prepared. While it is impractical to require that the disclosure statement be given to the buyer prior to delivery of the policy, it would be possible for the buyer (or the agent) to request the disclosure statement from the company prior to consummation of the sale. Furthermore, the "at or prior to delivery" requirement should be coupled with a "cooling-off period" of, say, ten days—measured from the date of delivery. During the cooling-off period the buyer would be able to cancel the policy and receive a refund of all premiums paid.

The information in the disclosure statement furnished to the buyer at or prior to delivery of the policy should be of two kinds: yearly and summary. The yearly information should be displayed in a columnar format, as illustrated in Table 1.

The first six columns are self-explanatory. The dividend figures are not guaranteed. The seventh column shows the amount of protection. This is based on the protection-savings view of cash-value life insurance under which it is assumed that the amount payable on surrender is considered properly as an asset of the policyholder.

The eighth column shows the yearly price per $1,000 of protection. This figure for any given year is calculated using the formula:

$$\frac{(P + CVP)(1 + i) - CVC - D}{(F - CVC)/(\$1,000)}$$

P is the yearly premium for the given year, CVP is the amount payable on surrender at the end of the preceding year, i is the assumed rate of return on the savings element expressed as a decimal, CVC is the amount payable on surrender at the end of the given year, D is the illustrated dividend for the given year, and F is the amount payable on death in the given year.

The yearly price figures in Table 1 are based on a five percent assumed rate of return on the savings element. This assumption was used because it approximates the interest rate currently being paid on many savings accounts and because the savings element of cash-value life insurance is similar to a savings account in many of its major characteristics. For example, the yearly price in the tenth policy year was calculated as follows:

$$\frac{(\$578 + \$3,862)(1 + .05) - \$4,331 - \$201}{(\$25,000 - \$4,331)/(\$1,000)} = \$6.29$$

In the calculation of the yearly prices, each year is treated as a separate entity. The figures are marginal yearly prices in a time sense because each figure reveals the price of continuing the protection for an additional year. The result is an extremely powerful form of disclosure. The relatively high price in the first policy year is a reflection of the front-end load. Starting in the second year the trend of the yearly prices is upward, reflecting the fact that the price per $1,000 of life insurance protection tends to increase with advancing age. In the particular policy illustrated, the yearly prices are relatively low in policy years two through nine and take a sharp jump in policy year ten.

The ninth column shows the rate of return on the savings element. This figure for any given policy year is calculated using the formula:

$$\frac{CVC + D + (YPM)(F - CVC)/(\$1,000)}{P + CVP} - 1$$

YPM is the assumed yearly price per $1,000 of protection in the given year and the other symbols are the same as those defined earlier.

The yearly rates of return in Table 1 are based on assumed yearly prices per $1,000 of protection equal to 105 percent of the one-year term insurance rates in Revenue Ruling 55-747. In the tenth policy year (at age 44), for example, the assumed yearly price per $1,000

23

TABLE 1
YEARLY INFORMATION

($25,000 Participating Straight-Life Policy Issued by Northwestern Mutual in 1973 to Males Aged 35)

(1) Policy Year	(2) Age at Beginning of Year	(3) Yearly Premium	(4) Amount Payable on Death	(5) Amount Payable on Surrender	(6) Illustrated Dividend[a]	(7) Amount of Protection[b]	(8) Yearly Price[c]	(9) Yearly Rate of Return[d]
1	35	$578	$25,000	$ 0	$ 69	$25,000	$21.51	---
2	36	578	25,000	449	83	24,551	3.09	---
3	37	578	25,000	912	96	24,088	2.91	---
4	38	578	25,000	1,384	110	23,616	3.00	6.69%
5	39	578	25,000	1,864	125	23,136	3.07	6.51
6	40	578	25,000	2,352	140	22,648	3.19	6.34
7	41	578	25,000	2,848	155	22,152	3.32	6.25
8	42	578	25,000	3,351	171	21,649	3.48	6.16
9	43	578	25,000	3,862	186	21,138	3.65	6.11
10	44	578	25,000	4,331	201	20,669	6.29	4.93
11	45	578	25,000	4,807	217	20,193	6.44	5.08
12	46	578	25,000	5,291	234	19,709	6.61	5.19
13	47	578	25,000	5,781	250	19,219	6.85	5.27
14	48	578	25,000	6,278	265	18,722	7.14	5.34
15	49	578	25,000	6,781	281	18,219	7.52	5.38
16	50	578	25,000	7,290	293	17,710	8.16	5.37
17	51	578	25,000	7,804	302	17,196	9.02	5.32
18	52	578	25,000	8,324	312	16,676	9.94	5.28
19	53	578	25,000	8,848	321	16,152	10.98	5.23
20	54	578	25,000	9,379	331	15,621	12.07	5.20

24

21	55	578	25,000	9,827	412	15,173	14.22	5.03
22	56	578	25,000	10,276	421	14,724	15.47	5.03
23	57	578	25,000	10,725	431	14,275	16.86	5.02
24	58	578	25,000	11,174	441	13,826	18.36	5.01
25	59	578	25,000	11,622	451	13,378	20.00	5.00
26	60	578	25,000	12,067	461	12,933	21.75	5.00
27	61	578	25,000	12,511	472	12,489	23.64	5.00
28	62	578	25,000	12,951	482	12,049	25.74	5.00
29	63	578	25,000	13,388	493	11,612	27.98	5.00
30	64	578	25,000	13,820	504	11,180	30.46	5.00
31	65	578	25,000	14,247	514	10,753	33.17	4.99
32	66	578	25,000	14,668	524	10,332	36.29	4.98
33	67	578	25,000	15,081	533	9,919	39.75	4.96
34	68	578	25,000	15,485	542	9,515	43.58	4.94
35	69	578	25,000	15,879	551	9,121	47.79	4.92
36	70	578	25,000	16,265	559	8,735	52.24	4.91
37	71	578	25,000	16,641	568	8,359	56.93	4.90
38	72	578	25,000	17,011	576	7,989	61.82	4.90
39	73	578	25,000	17,375	583	7,625	66.90	4.92
40	74	578	25,000	17,734	591	7,266	72.31	4.93

[a] Neither estimates nor guarantees, but merely illustrations of the company's 1973 dividend scale.
[b] Amount payable on death (col. 4) minus amount payable on surrender (col. 5).
[c] Yearly price per $1,000 of protection, assuming a 5% rate of return on the savings element.
[d] Yearly rate of return on the savings element, assuming yearly price per $1,000 of protection equal to 105% of the relevant one-year term insurance rate in Revenue Ruling 55-747.

of protection was $6.14. Thus, the 4.93 percent rate of return on the savings element in the tenth policy year was calculated as follows:

$$\frac{\$4,331 + \$201 + (\$6.14)(\$25,000 - \$4,331)/(\$1,000)}{\$578 + \$3,862} - 1 = .0493$$

Supplementing yearly prices with yearly rates of return should improve the effectiveness of the disclosure system as a communications device. The yearly price figures are fairly abstract; that is, a single yearly price figure in and of itself may not be meaningful to a buyer. For example, if the tenth year price per $1,000 of protection is $10.29 for a particular policy, this information is not meaningful unless accompanied by corresponding figures for other policies, by a one-year term insurance rate per $1,000 for the corresponding age, or by a death rate per 1,000 for the corresponding age. The yearly rates of return, on the other hand, may be meaningful because buyers are generally familiar with interest rates currently being paid on savings accounts in financial institutions. At the present time, for example, a 3.78 percent tenth year rate of return on the savings element for a particular policy is apt to be meaningful even if not accompanied by other data.

While yearly information is a vital part of an adequate system of life insurance disclosure, summary information is also needed to facilitate comparisons of similar policies. The summary information should be displayed as illustrated in Table 2.

The first figure in the table, the present expected value of the yearly premiums, is the single sum equivalent of the yearly premiums for the 40-year period, expressed as of the policy's issue date. The calculation takes into account both interest and probabilities of payment. The next three figures are the present expected values of, respectively, the protection element, the savings element, and the illustrated dividends.

The fifth figure is the present expected value of the company retention—what the company keeps to cover its expenses and make a profit—from the policyholder's viewpoint. This is the difference between what the policyholder pays in (the present expected value of the premiums) and what he gets back (the sum of the present expected values of the protection element, savings element, and illustrated dividends). When comparing similar policies issued by

TABLE 2

SUMMARY INFORMATION

($25,000 Participating Straight-Life Policy Issued by
Northwestern Mutual in 1973 to Males Aged 35)

Present expected values:[a]
    Premiums $6,899
    Components of the premiums:

Protection element	$1,149
Savings element	2,326
Illustrated dividends	2,575
Company retention	849

    Total...................................... $6,899

Supplementary premiums:

Waiver of premium	$ 110
Accidental death benefit	229

Annual percentage rates:

Semiannual premiums	8.2%
Quarterly premiums	8.0%
Monthly premiums	7.0%
Loan clause	6.0%

---

[a] The assumptions used in the calculation of these 40-year figures are 5% interest, the 1957-60 ultimate basic mortality table for males, and Moorhead's modified R lapse table.

different companies, a buyer should be interested in policies with relatively small retentions (see [3] for the formulas used in these calculations).

The next section of the table lists the present expected values of the premiums for various supplementary provisions. For the policy shown here, figures are given for the waiver-of-premium provision and the accidental death benefit. Other provisions that should be listed here if they are included in the policy would be a guaranteed insurability rider and a disability income rider.

The present expected value of the premiums in Table 2 is based on the assumption that premiums are paid yearly as are the data presented in Table 1. When premiums are paid more frequently, the life insurance company imposes carrying charges. Since the size of the carrying charges differs widely among companies, the added cost of semiannual, quarterly, and monthly premium payments should be disclosed. The information is shown in Table 2 in terms of annual percentage rates calculated with the tables provided by the Federal Reserve System for use in connection with the Truth-in-Lending Act.

The final item in Table 2 is the annual percentage rate provided for in the policy's loan clause. This is important because the policies of some companies provide for interest to be paid in advance. A stated interest rate of 6 percent payable in advance, for example, is equal to an annual percentage rate of 6.4 percent.

Summary information performs several important functions. First, it is useful when comparisons are being made among a large number of similar policies. For example, it would be impractical to examine carefully the detailed yearly information for the 163 participating policies and 166 nonparticipating policies for which company retentions are shown in Table 3. Information assembled in this manner illustrates the enormous variation among similar policies issued by different companies. The company retentions in Table 3, for example, range from $630 to $3,409 for the participating policies, and from $1,143 to $4,692 for the nonparticipating policies.

Second, summary information is helpful when the yearly information is inconclusive. For example, if the yearly prices for one policy are lower in some years and higher in others than for another similar policy, summary information (particularly the company retention figure) may help the buyer complete the comparison.

Third, summary information shows the relative importance of the protection and savings elements of the policy. For example, consider the $25,000 Northwestern Mutual straight-life policy for which summary information is shown in Table 2. The protection element of the policy has a value of $1,149 and the savings element has a value of $2,326.

TABLE 3

DISTRIBUTION OF SELECTED POLICIES
BY COMPANY RETENTIONS

($25,000 Participating and Nonparticipating Straight-Life Policies
Issued in 1973 to Males Aged 35 by Various Companies)

Company Retentions[a]	Number of Policies	
	Participating	Nonparticipating
$ 600 - $ 799	1	
800 - 999	8	
1,000 - 1,199	21	1
1,200 - 1,399	40	0
1,400 - 1,599	31	2
1,600 - 1,799	28	13
1,800 - 1,999	14	39
2,000 - 2,199	17	28
2,200 - 2,399	1	41
2,400 - 2,599	1	33
2,600 - 2,799	0	4
2,800 - 2,999	0	2
3,000 and over	1[b]	3[c]
Total policies	163	166

[a] Forty-year company retentions, assuming 5% interest, a modern select mortality table, and Moorhead's modified R lapse table.
[b] The company retention of this policy is $3,409.
[c] The company retentions of these policies are $3,375, $3,531, and $4,692.

Source: *Insurance Industry Pricing Study*, U.S. Senate Subcommittee on Antitrust and Monopoly, Wash., D.C.: U.S. Government Printing Office, 1974.

Periodic Disclosure

Virtually all of the discussion that has taken place concerning life insurance disclosure has dealt with point-of-sale disclosure.

Possibly as important, however, is the subject of periodic disclosure—preferably once each year—to the policyholder following the sale. The vehicle for periodic disclosure is available, since the information could be piggybacked on the premium notice sent to the policyholder on each yearly anniversary of the policy.

Some information is already given to the policyholder on a periodic basis. In some instances, however, only a bare minimum is provided—just enough so that the policyholder can pay the premium currently due and the company can record the payment. Such information usually consists of the policy number, the amount of the premium currently payable, the amount of the current dividend (in the case of a participating policy), and the amount of policy loan interest currently payable (if a policy loan is outstanding).

Certain additional information is essential to keep the policyholder informed of his situation. Perhaps most important is the price per $1,000 of protection for the past year and for the forthcoming year, and the rate of return on the savings element for the past year and for the forthcoming year. The assumptions used in the calculation of these figures would be those currently prescribed by the regulatory agency charged with the responsibility of administering the disclosure system.

Certain other information should also be disclosed to the policyholder periodically to remind him about the major provisions of his policy. The typical policyholder files away his policy as soon as he buys it and then rarely if ever looks at it again. Once a year, therefore, the insurance company should disclose the amount payable during the coming year in the event of the insured person's death, and the amount payable during the coming year in the event the policyholder surrenders the policy.

The company should also disclose the name of the beneficiary or beneficiaries currently designated to receive the proceeds of the policy in the event of the insured person's death. The company should include a warning to the policyholder if there are any restrictions in effect concerning the payment of death proceeds.

If the policy is participating the company should disclose each year certain information about the dividends. For example, if dividends are being left with the company to accumulate at interest, the periodic disclosure statement should show not only the amount of the current dividend, but also the amount of the fund currently, the amount of interest being added to the fund currently, and the interest rate currently being paid by the company on dividend accumulations (expressed as an annual percentage rate). Similarly, if dividends are being left with the company to purchase paid-up additions, the periodic disclosure statement should show not only the amount of the current dividend and the face amount of insurance being purchased with that dividend, but also the combined face amount and the combined cash value of all paid-up additions to the policy.

If there is a loan outstanding against the policy, the company should disclose each year not only the loan interest currently payable but also the current principal of the loan, and the interest rate currently being charged by the company on policy loans (expressed as an annual percentage rate). The latter item will become increasingly important as companies issue more and more new policies with variable policy loan interest rates.

Finally, the company should provide the name, address, and telephone number of: (1) the insurance agent (or other appropriate person) to be contacted if the policyholder has any questions about his policy, (2) the person to contact at the home office of the insurance company if the policyholder does not obtain satisfaction from the agent, and (3) the person to whom to complain in the state insurance commissioner's office if the policyholder does not obtain satisfaction from the insurance company.

CONCLUSION

The truth-in-life-insurance movement dates back to at least 1966. Among the major developments in the past decade were Senator Philip Hart's 1968 speech to a life insurance industry group, the report of the industry committee that was appointed shortly after Senator Hart's speech, the involvement of Mrs. Virginia Knauer, the activities of the National Association of Insurance Commissioners, the 1973 hearings conducted by Senator Hart and the introduction of S.2065 by Senator Hart in 1975.

31

The market for individual life insurance is characterized by a wide variety of deceptive sales practices. Many of these practices have one thing in common: the use of numbers (as opposed to adjectives and adverbs) combined in such a way as to give life insurance buyers and policyholders an erroneous impression of important relationships. Such practices usually result either in an understatement of the price of the life insurance protection element of a policy or in an overstatement of the rate of return on the savings element of a policy.

A rigorous system of disclosure is needed for the benefit of life insurance buyers and policyholders. Two forms of disclosure are necessary: point-of-sale and periodic. Point-of-sale disclosure should involve two kinds of information about the policy: yearly and summary. Yearly information should show yearly premiums, amounts payable on death, amounts payable on surrender, illustrated dividends, amounts of protection, yearly prices and yearly rates of return. Summary information should show the breakdown of the premiums into their four components: the protection element, the savings element, the illustrated dividends and the company retention. Periodic disclosure should include current yearly price information, current yearly rate-of-return information, and other relevant information to keep the policyholder informed of the status of his policy.

REFERENCES

1. Belth, Joseph M. "Deceptive Sales Practices in the Life Insurance Business," *Journal of Risk and Insurance,* 41 (June 1974), 305-26.

2. _____. "Information Disclosure to the Life Insurance Consumer," *Drake Law Review,* 24 (Dec. 1975), 727-52.

3. _____. *Life Insurance: A Consumer's Handbook.* Bloomington: Indiana Univ. Press, 1973, 236-7.

4. _____. *The Retail Price Structure in American Life Insurance.* Bloomington, Ind.: Bureau of Business Research, Graduate School of Business, Indiana Univ., 1966, 239.

5. "Big Gap in Life Insurance Costs Found in Study by Pennsylvania," *New York Times* (Apr. 19, 1972), 1, 14.

6. Brinton, Dilworth C. "Counters Buy Term Invest the Rest Argument at NALU Annual," *National Underwriter,* NALU convention daily/life-health ed. (Sept. 16, 1970), 10, 12-14.

7. "Complete Text of Hart's Remarks on Life Insurance 'Truth' Proposal," *National Underwriter,* life ed. (Mar. 16, 1974), 1.

8. *Cost Facts on Life Insurance: Interest Adjusted Method.* Cincinnati, Ohio: National Underwriter Co., 1970.

9. "Digest of Discussion of Subjects of Special Interest," *Transactions of the Society of Actuaries,* 14 (1962), D353-5.

10. Federal Trade Commission. *National Consumer Protection Hearings,* November 1968. Washington, D.C.: U.S. Government Printing Office, 1969.

11. Gaines, Price, Jr. "ALIA Position on Costs: Work for Interest-Adjusted Method," *National Underwriter,* life ed. (Mar. 9, 1974), 1, 24-25.

12. _____. "Nader Indicts Life Industry before Senate," *National Underwriter,* life ed. (Feb. 24, 1973), 1-2.

13. _____. "Senate Unit's Questions Hint at Feelings on Life Ins. Costs," *National Underwriter,* life ed. (Mar. 10, 1973), 1-2.

14. _____. "Senate Urged to Change Controls on Life Costs," *National Underwriter,* life ed. (Mar. 3, 1973), 1, 26.

15. _____. "Sen. Hart Holds Housekeeping Session on Life Ins. Industry," *National Underwriter,* life ed. (July 20, 1974), 1, 23.

16. _____ and Linda Kocolowski. "NAIC Unit Backs Bill Requiring I-A Method," *National Underwriter,* life ed. (June 9, 1973), 1, 4-5.

17. _____ and Thomas M. Maher. "Sen. Hart Says He's Drafting 'Truth in Life Insurance' Bill," *National Underwriter,* life ed. (Mar. 9, 1974), 1, 24-25.

18. Harris, Richard F., Jr. "I Tell Corporations, 'Put the Difference in Permanent,'" *Life Insurance Selling,* 45 (Feb. 1970), 24-6, 28.

19. "Hart Introduces 'Truth in Life Insurance' Measure," *National Underwriter,* life ed. (July 12, 1975), 1, 5.

20. "Hart Warns of 'Truth in Life Insurance' Bill," *National Underwriter,* life ed. (Oct. 26, 1968), 15, 20-1.

21. "Lee Shield on Wage-Price Freeze, National Health Care, Consumerism," *National Underwriter,* life ed. (Nov. 6, 1971), 13-4, 26-7.

22. *The Life Insurance Industry,* Hearings before the Subcommittee on Antitrust and Monopoly of the Committee on the Judiciary, Parts 1-3, U.S. Senate, 93rd Cong., 1st sess. Washington, D.C.: U.S. Government Printing Office, 1973.

23. *The Life Insurance Industry.* Hearings before the Subcommittee on Antitrust and Monopoly of the Committee on the Judiciary, Part 4, U.S. Senate, 93rd Cong., 2nd sess. Washington, D.C.: U.S. Government Printing Office, 1974.

24. Macfarlane, William. "Belth Introduces Broad Policy Information Disclosure System," *National Underwriter,* life ed. (May 13, 1972), 1, 4-6.

25. "Mrs. Knauer Presses Insurers to Act on Cost Comparison Changes—and Soon," *National Underwriter,* life ed. (Sept 18, 1971), 1, 31.

26. *Report of the Joint Special Committee on Life Insurance Costs.* New York: Institute of Life Insurance, 1970.

27. Sesser, Stanford. "Critics Say Practices of Industry Confuse Life Insurance Buyers," *Wall Street Journal* (Sept. 5, 1967), 1, 22.

28. *A Shopper's Guide to Life Insurance.* Harrisburg, Pa.: Pennsylvania Insurance Department, 1972.

29. *Wisconsin Administrative Code,* Sec. Ins 2.15.

30. Wolfe, Wayne W. *See You Next Week.* Indianapolis, Ind.; Research and Review Service of America, 1968, 74-5.

CONSUMER PRODUCT LABELING—AN EVALUATION
OF RESEARCH OPPORTUNITIES

Benjamin J. Katz
School of Business Administration
Philadelphia College of Textiles & Science

Katz argues for the need to measure and predict the effectiveness of product label information mandated by various government agencies. He reviews previous research efforts in this direction and points out the weaknesses of these efforts. He then presents some new approaches that might be more fruitful in evaluating product labeling regulations.

The importance of government actions regarding product labeling derives from the historical role of labeling in government regulation of marketing practices and from the recent proliferation of new labeling rules and requirements. It should be noted that the first of the series of major pieces of consumer legislation that emerged from Congress in the 1960s was the much-debated Hart Bill. This eventually became law as the "Fair Packaging and Labeling Act," popularly known as the "Truth-in-Packaging Law."

INTRODUCTION

Much has been written about the felt need in public affairs for more consumer product information. In studying the effects of product information on consumer behavior, Jacoby observed that consumer advocates and government regulators in Congress and the federal agencies continue to issue a call for "full and open disclosure." They reflect the common belief that "complete information," with more labeling on more types of goods, will result in consumers making more rational choices and "correct purchase decisions" [9]. Also, referring to the problems of consumerism, several marketing scholars have contended that programs to supply more consumer product information represent the best solution to widespread consumer disappointment [8, 20].

As a result of the growing pressure from consumer advocates and others, the government has tried to respond to the demand for more labeling [7, 17]. A recent analysis of government actions listed in seven separate government publications and marketing references on consumer affairs derived a sample set of 225 federal statutes, congressional bills and administrative agency regulations. Of the 225 government actions, a total of 64 (or 28.4 percent) were identified as "product labeling regulations." Labeling regulations comprised the largest category of all government consumer regulations. It appears that, for the government official, labeling is a simple and actionable response to various consumer complaints about product purchase disappointments [13].

Need for Measurement

With the rapid growth in government activity in the field of consumer product information, many observers have called for the application of consumer research methods to measure the results of such actions. In 1968 David Gardner suggested that more consumer legislation should be preceded by practical consumer research [6]. Mary Gardiner Jones called on the research community to contribute to more sophisticated methods of planning and executing consumer regulation programs at the Federal Trade Commission [11]. Others have recommended that the government use the same management science techniques that have helped business managers in the private sector to predict the effects of their advertising and labeling programs; thus, government policymakers could choose among alternative expenditures of money and effort by using the results of consumer tests as decision model inputs.

However, it has not proved easy to put marketing research to work on behalf of public policy decision makers. Wilkie and Cohen have warned of the problems involved when psychologists and scientists begin to interact with lawyer-type thinking, with its advocacy tradition. Lawyers are trained to prove a case on the basis of a prior assumed position. The adversary method used in court trials and carried over into legislative and administrative hearing rooms does not encourage objective evaluation [22]. More recently, Gardner has cautioned researchers and academics to become involved with the government process first and then to involve government-client personnel in the research planning [5].

Management and Government

The difficulties of introducing surveys and consumer experiments into the planning and decision-making process for government regulation of marketing practices are reminiscent of the difficulties endured by pioneers in the early days of commercial market research. Managers often favored those surveys that lent support to their own biases. Eventually, market researchers began to urge their colleagues to involve the research user (i.e., the client or sales manager) in their planning. The object was to design research projects whose results would be used and not ignored by the firm's management.

The same call for understandable research methods and actionable research results is now being heard in the field of public policy toward marketing. As Wilkie and Gardner stated: "Policy makers are decision makers. They are not interested in theory; they want practical, useful information." [23] To be useful, test results on product information must be relatively free of criticism as to their external validity. Unrealistic experimental conditions are viewed by government lawyers as relatively useless in predicting what their consumer constituents will do in their day-to-day shopping.

The research work published to date on consumer product information has stressed the more general, more idealistic, and more theoretical approach. It lacks the more specific, more practical, and more useful results and conclusions needed to fit regulators' decision models. This means researchers must do more than question, as Wilkie has already done, the applicability of the older information-processing research and the theories developed by communication psychologists working outside the marketing area. It means that the marketing researchers' own recent tests of unit pricing, freshness dating, and nutritional labeling have not suited the needs of the regulators and have not been understood.

One type of social research that any Washington legislator or bureaucrat can understand is a public opinion poll. Therefore, sur-

veys to measure *actual recall or preference* for alternative information items printed on *real product labels* are easier to explain than
the results of laboratory experiments on hypothetical product
attributes (or information cues) typed on index cards.

FOUR ASPECTS OF LABELING RESEARCH

This article is based on a study of the testability of over sixteen
different labeling regulations currently in effect or proposed by government agencies. It examines the changes that might be helpful in
four areas related to consumer research on product labels.

First, it behooves us to review the various product classes so that
the government's judgment of the usefulness and importance of
consumer research will not be based on studies involving "unimpor-
tant" products. Second, we must analyze the effects, or criterion
variables, that the regulator would want measured to explain whether
or not he had achieved his intended purpose through a specific new
labeling requirement.

Third, we will examine a set of predictor variables or controllable
policy factors that might be associated with the regulators' own
measures of effectiveness. These should be the factors that can be
manipulated to help develop alternative labeling programs in the
future.

Fourth, the types of consumer samples that have been used in
early experiments in university settings must be superseded by the
realistic collection of responses from a sufficient number of buyers
in the field.

Researchers aware of these four problem areas may then consider
which of the existing product labeling regulation cases might lend
themselves best to research using measures of the chosen criterion
variables, given the possibility of setting various levels of the policy
factors by government action.

Selection of Regulation-Prone Products

The test items used in earlier studies of the effects of product
labeling rules frequently were selected because of their *convenience*
to the researcher rather than their *interest value* for regulators. Many
consumer packaged goods sold in food markets are not "information-

intensive." Buyers who ignore nutritional label information on supermarket food items might pay more attention to information about automobiles, tires, television sets, or household electrical appliances.

The factors affecting the extent of a buyer's search include elements in the profile of the buyer as well as characteristics of the product and the buying situation [3, 19]. Information is sought to reduce the uncertainty and risk associated with the purchase. One type of risk is financial risk associated with the absolute price of the product and with the proportion of the product's annual cost relative to the family's annual household budget. Risk to health and safety, and risk of embarrassment in social situations, are also factors in some products. Consequently, the risk on low-priced grocery products may be perceived as considerably less than that of relatively high-priced durable goods, and this perception of risk will be reflected in the amount of attention paid to labeling information.

Academic research on label effects may tend to focus on grocery products if the support funds for the research come from organizations interested in such products. Yet, if it is found that label information does not significantly change buyer behavior in choosing brands in the case, for example, of a package of rice, the regulator may feel it is because rice is not an "important" purchase compared to a car, or a set of steel-belted radial tires, or a new coffee maker. When buyers of packaged rice, or light bulbs, or other non-information-intensive products are shown to have ignored labeling, the government regulator may still want to know the effects in cases that he has worked on or heard about in Washington.

Regulators and government lawyers are more likely to be interested in, and impressed by, tests of the effectiveness of product information requirements on the following items: (1) used-car disclosure stickers; (2) automobile tire treadwear and traction labeling; (3) gasoline octane posting; (4) electric appliance energy efficiency labels; and (5) warning labels on dangerous household cleaning products. These five items might be among the better, more realistic candidates for products on which we can base labeling studies. They have already been selected for special regulatory attention in recent or proposed information requirements by the Federal Trade Commission, the Department of Transportation, or the Consumer Product Safety Commission. These items apparently are considered important by the government.

40

Criterion Variables for Public Policy Effectiveness

Having observed that the contributions of empirical research to public policy in product labeling may be meager unless studies are conducted on products considered important by regulators, let us next examine the types of label effectiveness tests in terms of their objective function concepts. What effects should be measured to help regulators predict and influence the results of label rules?

Measuring the effectiveness of government labeling information requirements may be viewed as analogous to the much-discussed question of measuring the effectiveness of advertising programs by marketing firms. Colley contends that to measure advertising results one must define advertising goals. The goal may be to affect sales or behavioral objectives, or to affect communications or attitudinal objectives [2]. The model developed by Lavidge and Steiner in their study of advertising effects measurements has relevance for measuring the effects of product labeling [15]. This model suggests that "higher effects," such as purchase (behavioral) or preference (attitudinal), might be preceded by "cognitive effects," beginning with *awareness* of the product and *knowledge* of product information and facts.

The effects of labeling, like the effects of advertising, are varied, complex, and interactive. In business, the marketing policymaker may want his advertising program to result in a greater volume of sales of a given product; yet he may measure the effectiveness of his advertising in terms of "brand awareness" or "message recall." In government, the public policymaker may want his labeling program to result in fewer complaints about sales of a given product type, but he may have to measure the effectiveness of his regulations in terms of "awareness," "knowledge," or "utilization" of the product labeling information. It may not be feasible to measure the effect of labeling on consumer choice behavior, satisfaction, dissatisfaction, disappointment, or complaint levels.

Table 1 presents the levels in a hierarchy of effects for labeling regulation. For a government decision process model, the "ideal measure" would be a dependent variable that reflected the objective of the decision maker (i.e., the government agency or regulator). One study suggested that the objective function for the government might

41

TABLE 1
A HIERARCHY OF CRITERION MEASURES OF
LABELING REGULATION EFFECTIVENESS

Criterion	Basis
Awareness	Labeling information noticed by or expected by the buyer
Knowledge	Material facts and descriptive information understood
Utilization	Information applied to choice behavior in the buyer's decision process
Consumer benefit	Use of the information resulted in increased purchase value satisfaction
Government objective	Consumer benefits resulted in minimizing disappointment and buyer complaints

be to minimize the level of "purchase value shortfall" for a given product class [12]. This shortfall measure is a type of nondiscrete disappointment measure. In practice, lacking consumer research data on expected purchase value and realized purchase value, many government agencies assume that the level of complaints adequately reflects disappointment; they use actual complaint count proportions as a surrogate measure of the effectiveness of consumer regulations [4, 24].

For a management science approach to selecting the best of the existing government labeling proposals, the government's operational objective measure must be defined and used to compare predicted effects or observed effects. While this is the ideal measure, it is not the measure used by researchers. In the tests of labeling information effects published to date, the dependent variables have been what may be termed "traditional measures." These measures are carried over and borrowed from the managerial models. The effects on buyer response in terms of brand choice or brand perception have been used, for example, in tests of unit pricing information and nutritional labeling [1, 16].

42

In dealing with public policy matters, some researchers assume that a relevant dependent variable might be associated with the consumer's satisfaction or preference map ideal point. Jacoby and his associates used such a measure in their studies of "information overload" [10]. They used labeling information presented on index cards to a sample of simulated buyers in a laboratory experiment. The dependent variable, "Most Preferred Brand Accuracy," was defined in terms of the closeness of the subject's "best" brand choice to the subject's "ideal" brand description. By this measure, the regulator would have to decide if the buyers tended to choose their "best" brand more frequently with or without the labeling information. A consultant might have some trouble convincing his government regulator client about the external validity of tests using traditional dependent variables of this type.

Many regulators might prefer to obtain the answers to the following questions:

"Did buyers notice the information?" (awareness)
"Did they understand the information?" (knowledge)
"Did they use the information in making their purchase decisions?" (utilization)

Information is not likely to be used and to have its intended effect unless it is first attended to by the buyer and understood clearly [21]. It is reasonable to assume that labeling regulation anticipates that the buyer will at least be aware of the information on the label. If consumer research indicates that there is no significant change in the level of awareness of the material facts after the labeling treatment has exposed these facts for a sufficient time, one must conclude that the labeling treatment did not have its intended effect.

Therefore, it seems that instead of the "ideal measure," which is not available, or the "traditional measures," which do not fit the government's needs, researchers interested in the effects of product labeling might choose a dependent variable (or criterion variable) from among the "operational measures"—awareness, knowledge, or utilization of label information. These consequences of labeling requirements are practical and appear to be necessary prerequisites to goal-related results.

Determinants of Labeling Effectiveness

For public purposes, it is important to measure the factors the government can control. The factors that may be associated with differences or changes in labeling effects include a wide array of independent variables (or predictor variables) for the labeling information model. But a decision process model for government officials must feature policy variables that the government can promulgate, legislate, regulate, and manipulate in labeling requirements.

Most studies of label effects relate to only one factor: the presence or absence of the labeling information. Yet there are many different kinds of controllable factors that might contribute to the effectiveness of a labeling requirement. Table 2 gives a partial review of some elements to be considered in selecting independent variables for label effects tests. The key is to focus research designs on factors that the regulator finds useful for improving labeling regulation effectiveness. This results in actionable research for government.

Label Display Format

A detailed discussion of what makes people notice or look for label information is not required here. However, we must note that published research has generally not given us test results related to how the labeling information can best be presented physically to increase awareness and utilization levels. Government lawyers often try to specify type sizes and label formats, but the real experts on label design are the professional graphic communicators. Advertising artists, graphic designers, and creative printers can provide new ways to either emphasize or subdue the awareness of a given label under any regulation requirement. It is not enough for the government to require that the labeling information be *present*; the label display *formats* should be tested using well-developed consumer perception measures familiar to package designers in large marketing organizations.

One study, conducted in New Jersey on the FTC light bulb labeling rule, indicated that the product's labeling information was not used or even noticed [14]. It might have drawn more attention, though, if the package designer had been instructed to assure that the

TABLE 2

FACTORS RELATED TO LABELING
REGULATION EFFECTIVENESS

Label Factors	Display format:
	Graphics (e.g., type size, proportion of type area to total display area)
	Wording (e.g., characterizing ingredients listed in decreasing order of weight, versus tabular listing of ingredients with numerical statement of measure for each item)
	Total design of label for communications effectiveness
	Source of information:
	Seller
	Government agency (e.g., USDA, NBS)
	Consumer organization (e.g., Consumers Union)
	Directness of information:
	Evaluative indicators (rating numbers, grade labeling)
	Descriptive indicators (attribute labeling, quality cues)
Product Information— Intensity Factors	Perceived risk
	Value and cost of information search
	Importance of purchase
	Confidence in choice
Buyer Information— Sensitivity Factors	Consumer education
	Selective information perception
	Information-processing capacity
	Situation of purchase or product usage

required information was featured. Research could provide pretests of alternative graphic design formats and alternative wording methods. In the light bulb case, the quality indicator for the brightness or light output of the light bulb was stated in number of "lumens" [18]. The regulation required that the word *lumens* be used, and that it be followed by the words *light output* in parentheses for only the first year after the rule became effective. This requirement was conceived in the minds of some FTC lawyers. A marketing communications expert would probably have taken a different approach. When requiring the presentation of information, the government must ensure that it is communicated effectively if the information is to be utilized as intended.

Acceptably Representative Samples

Government lawyers are usually not trained in sampling theory, statistical analysis and the methods used by social scientists and consumer psychologists. They may tend to ignore the results of studies based on what they perceive as a small group of students or special people chosen by a researcher in a college town. The regulator, instead, wants a report on what a large number of typical consumers actually did or said.

This means we need adequate samples of respondents who are really buyers in real stores or other actual field situations, to make the research results acceptable and "practical" for the government client.

SUMMARY

With the growing consumerists' demands for product information and the proliferation of congressional bills, statutes, and federal agency regulations requiring specific labeling information, came a call for the application of consumer research techniques to the goverment regulation decision process. The need to measure and predict the effectiveness of labeling activity was expressed by those who felt it would help produce more rational and efficient public policy toward marketing and consumers.

Recently there has been some criticism of the types of experiments and surveys undertaken by researchers concerned with consumer product information, including package labeling. There are complaints that this research, particularly in the academic sector, tends to be too general, too theoretical, and too artificial to be accepted and used by government policymakers. Warnings have been voiced that the research will not be actionable unless and until researchers understand and respond to the specific needs and customary operations of the regulators who may make use of their findings.

An overview of the current state of consumer research applied to product labeling regulation suggests that new research efforts might be more readily integrated into public policy if different approaches were taken in the selection of the following four elements:

1. Product classes—information-intensive products, high in complaints (e.g., automobile tires, used cars)
2. Criterion variables—measures of effects directly related to objectives of the regulator (e.g., awareness of label information)
3. Policy variables—rule requirements readily defined (e.g., label display formats and graphics)
4. Consumer samples—typical buyers in realistic field situations, with large sample sizes

Some product label regulation research seeks to determine whether consumers have somehow benefited from the addition of the label information. Another approach would be to test whether consumer awareness of the label information is greater with one display format than with other formats. Research projects in this field can be designed so that their results help develop better working relationships between consumer researchers and government lawyers.

REFERENCES

1. Asam, E. H. and L. P. Bucklin. "Nutritional Labeling for Canned Goods: A Study of Consumer Response," *Journal of Marketing,* 37 (Apr. 1973), 32-7.

2. Colley, Russell H. *Defining Advertising Goals for Measured Advertising Results.* New York: Assn. of National Advertisers, 1961.

3. Engel, J. S., D. T. Kollat, and R. D. Blackwell. *Consumer Behavior.* New York: Holt Rinehart & Winston, 1968.

4. Gaedeke, Ralph M. "Filing and Disposition of Consumer Complaints: Some Empirical Evidence," *Journal of Consumer Affairs,* (Summer 1972), 45-56.

5. Gardner, David M. "Dynamic Homeostasis: Behavioral Research and the FTC," in Scott Ward and Peter Wright, eds., *Proceedings of the Association for Consumer Research.* 1973, 108-13.

6. _____. "The Package, Legislation, and the Shopper," *Business Horizons* (Oct. 1968), 53-8.

7. Hicks, Lawrence E. *Product Labeling and the Law.* New York: MACON Division, American Management Assn., 1974.

8. Holton, Richard H. "Government-Consumer Interest: Conflicts and Prospects," in Reed Moyer, ed., *Proceedings of the American Marketing Association 1967 Winter Conference.* Chicago: American Marketing Assn., 1967.

9. Jacoby, Jacob. "Consumer Reaction to Information Displays: Packaging and Advertising," in S. F. Divita, ed., *Advertising and the Public Interest.* Chicago: American Marketing Assn., 1974.

10. _____, D. Speller, and C. Cohn. "Brand Choice Behavior as a Function of Information Load: Replication and Extension," *Journal of Consumer Research,* (June 1974).

11. Jones, Mary Gardiner. "The FTC's Need for Social Science Research," in *Proceedings of the Second Annual Conference, Assn. for Consumer Research.* 1971, 1-9.

12. Katz, Benjamin J. "The Objective Measure for a Government Regulation Decision Model in Marketing," in Robert W. Hall,

ed., *Proceedings of the American Institute for Decision Sciences Midwest Conference.* Indianapolis, Ind., 1975, 400-4.

13. _____. "Public Policy Toward Consumer Product Information" (Ph.D. diss., University of Pennsylvania, 1974), 232.

14. _____ and J. A. Rose. "Information Utilization and the Awareness Criterion in Labeling Regulation," in Kenneth L. Bernhardt, ed., *1976 Educators Proceedings.* Chicago: American Marketing Assn., 1976.

15. Lavidge, R. J. and G. A. Steiner. "A Model for Predictive Measurements of Advertising Effectiveness," *Journal of Marketing,* 25 (Oct. 1961), 61.

16. McCullough, T. D. and D. I. Padberg. "Unit Pricing in Supermarkets: Alternatives, Costs, and Consumer Reaction," *Search,* 1 (Jan. 1971).

17. National Business Council for Consumer Affairs. *Guiding Principles for Responsible Packaging and Labeling.* Washington, D.C.: U.S. Department of Commerce, 1972.

18. "New Labels on Light Bulbs," *Consumer Bulletin,* 54 (Apr. 1971), 34-6.

19. Ross, Ivan. "Applications of Consumer Information to Public Policy Decisions," in J. N. Sheth and P. L. Wright, eds., *Marketing Analysis for Societal Problems.* Urbana-Champaign: University of Illinois, 1974.

20. Stern, Louis L. "Consumer Protection Via Increased Information," *Journal of Marketing,* 31 (Apr. 1967), 48-52.

21. Wilkie, William L. *How Consumers Use Product Information: An Assessment of Research in Relation to Public Policy Needs.* Washington, D.C.: National Science Foundation, 1975.

22. _____ and J. B. Cohen. "You, Too, Can Do FTC Consumer-Oriented Studies," *Marketing News,* 9 (Jan. 16, 1976), 9, 23.

23. _____ and D. M. Gardner. "The Role of Marketing Research in Public Policy Decision Making," *Journal of Marketing,* 38 (Jan. 1974), 38-47.

24. Wilson, Jane S., ed. "Complaint Letters to Virginia Knauer's Office," *Of Consuming Interest,* 5 (July 10, 1972).

PART 2

Consumer Product Safety

CONSUMER PRODUCT SAFETY: STRATEGIES FOR REDUCING THE INCIDENCE OF PRODUCT-RELATED INJURIES

Richard Staelin
Carnegie Mellon University

R. D. Pittle
U.S. Consumer Product Safety Commission

This paper addresses the issue of consumer product–related injuries. The authors first discuss a method for determining the effectiveness of a product safety program, and then look at the reasons for many product-related injuries and examine consumer behavior vis à vis the safety factor as it affects a purchase decision. Finally, proposals are offered for reducing the incidence of such injuries.

Annually one out of every ten persons in the U.S. suffers a consumer product–related injury requiring professional medical attention or resulting in one or more days of restricted activity. Yet, there is little agreement with respect to the best approach for reducing the magnitude of these injuries. Three major avenues have been proposed: Two stress the supply side and place the responsibility either on industry to produce safe products voluntarily or on government to mandate adequate safety, while the third is concerned with the demand side and with influencing consumer behavior so that consumers purchase safer products and use products more safely.

Each of these three approaches implicitly assumes a different model of consumer behavior. To put it another way, if we knew more about how the consumer purchases and uses consumer products with respect to safety, we could better appraise the likelihood of success for each approach. For instance, in a world where customers have perfect information about product risks and are able to process this information correctly, there is no need for a government agency to regulate safety, since in theory the free market system insures safety standards that optimally balance the value associated with the reduction of accidents and the costs associated with the increased expense of safer designs. In contrast, if consumers place little importance on safety or are unaware of the true risks involved in purchasing or using a product, there is no economic reason for manufacturers to consider safety an important feature in a product's design. Consequently, if injuries are to be reduced through product design, a third party, usually the government, must replace the market forces to ensure that manufacturers produce safe products.

In this paper, we will first review a method for analyzing the efficacy of any proposed approach to consumer product safety. Then, after discussing a number of studies of consumer safety use and purchase behavior, we will use the framework of the proposed methodology to assess the adequacy of numerous suggestions for reducing consumer product-related injuries.

METHOD FOR MEASURING EFFICACY
OF SAFETY PROGRAMS

Any methodology aimed at determining the adequacy of different approaches to product safety should consider the costs associated with reducing the number of accidents as well as the benefits derived from these reductions. This can be done within the framework of a standard cost-benefit analysis. For example, Lave analyzed the costs of certain automobile safety features required on all 1968 automobiles and compared these costs to the expected benefits [9]. To calculate the expected benefits, he first estimated the number of injuries by type (i.e., fatal, dangerous, minor, etc.) that were avoided because of the specific safety features. Then, using a weighting scheme that equates the severity of each type of injury relative to a fatal injury, and the dollar cost to society for a human fatality, he calculated the expected dollar benefit for each safety feature. In other words, he multiplied the monetary value for avoiding each type of injury by the frequency of these avoided injuries and then summed over all types of injuries to get an aggregate measure of benefit. The derived benefit was then compared to the cost to

54

society in terms of incremental price increases associated with the safety feature to determine the cost-benefit ratio. Michaels and Shanker conducted a similar type of analysis for bicycles [11]. They used the Consumer Product Safety Commission's (CPSC) estimates of the frequency of occurrence of each type of bike injury as well as the commission's original weighting scheme which measures the relative severity of each type of injury. This latter input, coupled with an estimate of the value of a human life (as measured by the discounted cash flow of earnings over the worker's lifetime), allowed them to estimate the monetary value of avoiding each type of injury. The results indicated that if product modifications could reduce the expected injury costs to zero, these modifications would be cost-effective provided they added less than $16.50 to the price of each bicycle. Likewise, if the probability of injury was reduced by a uniform 25 percent over all classes of injury, this reduction would be justified provided the added production costs did not exceed $4.12 per bike.

These analyses require that the decision maker place a specific monetary value on the loss of a statistical human life. Although one might argue on philosophical terms that a life has infinite value, it is clear that in practice most decision makers implicitly assume some finite limit. For example, when funds are allocated for road construction, a limited budget normally precludes the design and installation of the safest possible median barriers. Likewise, Congress does not fund the Food and Drug Administration adequately to allow them to inspect every batch of food, even though it is probable that these inspection limitations will result in the sale of some contaminated foods that will lead to a loss of human life. Consequently, the critical question is: How much are we as a society willing to pay to lower the probability of an injury or death by a specified amount? Individual decision makers generally have different feelings about the conceptual value of human life.

The above two studies used only the loss of anticipated earnings. Others have suggested that the imputed costs of pain and suffering should be included. Recently, Conley showed that it is theoretically superior to use the "willingness to pay" method rather than the above-referenced human capital approach [1]. The willingness-to-pay method is based on a theoretical model of individual behavior and assumes that a consumer chooses that activity (product) in any period to maximize total expected lifetime utility subject to a budget constraint. Conley's major conclusion is that for most income levels the value of life is greater than discounted earnings, and in early and middle adulthood it is greater than discounted consumption. Thus, cost-benefit analyses that use discounted earnings may understate the benefit of the safety program.

Regardless of the value used, once this parameter has been set, the rest of the analysis is straightforward. This is especially true now that the CPSC collects and publishes reasonably accurate estimates of the frequency of occurrence of each type of consumer product–related injury (receiving hospital emergency treatment) by product class. Thus, the only other inputs required are: (a) the value of a human life, (b) a weighting scheme to take into account the severity of the type of injury, and (c) estimates of the degree to which a program can reduce the occurrence of each type of injury. These inputs, although somewhat controversial, are no more difficult to estimate than the types of input required of, say, a marketing manager using a decision-calculus–type model [10] who wants to assess the value of a particular advertising budget or sales force call plan. Considering the magnitude of the costs associated with many of the proposed safety plans, it would seem worthwile to subject these plans to a rigorous cost-benefit analysis.

Finally, it should be noted that most cost-benefit analyses estimate the costs to be the amount of extra money paid by consumers for the safety program. However, safety programs in general increase the price of the product class. Thus, they also may alter the demand between product classes, since in general some consumers will switch their consumption because of the price change. Theoretically, this shift in demand cannot increase the consumer's welfare (utility), and most likely it will result in a welfare reduction. Consequently, any proposed program that leads to increased prices should also be evaluated in terms of shifts in demand (i.e., the loss in utility associated with the forced shift in consumption patterns). Estimating the cost of this shift is nontrivial; it may be best handled preliminarily in a qualitative fashion.

The above methodology is useful in assessing the efficacy of *any* approach to safety, not just safety standards established by regulation. For example, government-sponsored consumer education and the dissemination of product safety information have been proposed as possible methods of reducing injuries [15]. Although this paper will not conduct specific cost-benefit analyses for these two approaches, some attempt will be made, using general marketing theory and studies in consumer behavior, to assess the value of these and other methods.

CAUSES OF INJURY

Before we can meaningfully discuss solutions to reducing the magnitude of product-related injuries, we must first understand how such injuries occur. As the term *product-related* implies, injuries by definition are associated with the interaction of a consumer and a product. More specifically, it would be useful to know what percentage of the injuries are caused by a faulty or unsafe product, what percentage are caused by the consumer misusing or abusing a normally safe product, and what percentage are attributable to a combination of the two factors.

At least three studies have broken the problem down in this manner. Tokuhata studied the circumstances surrounding the injuries of 2,753 children treated in emergency rooms at six central Pennsylvania hospitals over a one-year period [19]. Over 75 percent of the injuries occurred in the home and involved common consumer products such as bicycles, electric irons, knives, and furniture. No criteria for classification of injuries were given, but Tokuhata concluded that 2 percent of the injuries were caused solely by defects in the consumer products, 18 percent were partially caused by the product, and 40 percent were entirely caused by the consumer who misused the product. In 86 percent of the cases, the human factor contributed significantly to the injury, although it is not clear from the report whether better product design might have prevented its occurrence. A second study was reported by Whitaker in a statement before the House Subcommittee on Commerce and Finance [20]. He estimated that between 5 and 20 percent of consumer product—related injuries and deaths were avoidable through improved product design or safety standards.

Finally, a recent CPSC study analyzed the in-depth investigation reports of over 2,500 injuries associated with products in 47 product categories [3]. The study concluded that "the weighted average percent of product injury due to product failure over all 47 product categories considered was found to be approximately 10 percent," and "the weighted average percent of injuries addressable by standards in the samples studied was found to be approximately 20 percent." The estimates by product class differed substantially. For example, the commission estimated that 14 percent of all injuries associated with bicycles (or 64,000 injuries annually) are addressable by a standard. The respective figure for glass soft drink bottles is 53 percent (or 23,800 injuries annually), while for unpowered cutlery the numbers are 0 percent and 0 injuries annually. In determining these estimates, the study assumed that if a standard could have saved the injury, the injury was addressable. Thus, for example, in analyzing snowmobile-related injuries it was felt that many of these injuries would have been avoided if there had been a standard requiring seat belts *and if the consumer had used these belts.* All of these injuries were considered to be addressable by standards, even though there was no guarantee that the consumer would use the seat belt or whatever provided by the standard. Thus, the 20 percent probably should be viewed as CPSC's most optimistic estimate of the percentage of injuries that could be avoided through the use of standards.

All of the above studies used different data bases and somewhat different methodologies to classify the causes of injury. Even so, they all reached the same general conclusion: that standards and/or regulations are capable of solving only a minority of consumer product-related injuries. Turning this statement around, we note that the vast majority of injuries, if they are to be reduced, must be addressed through changes in consumer behavior. Despite this evidence, most safety research as well as government regulatory activity is associated with setting standards or otherwise altering the supply of products—an approach that at best can solve only 20 percent of the problem.

It is interesting to speculate why so much effort is spent on the "tip of the iceberg." One reason seems to be that safety standards, although difficult to write, represent a well-defined task directly connected with injury avoidance. Similarly, there is an immediate impact on injury reduction when a hazardous product is removed from the marketplace through a recall or ban. In contrast, there is no

58

clearcut method for altering consumers' safety behavior. The causal links between injury and behavior are not well defined. Also, there is much evidence that consumers are inefficient processors of information [e.g., 5, 16]. Thus, much less action has been taken in consumer behavior modification. More generally, if effective consumer-related programs are to be implemented, it is essential that planners have a good understanding of those factors that influence the behavior of interest. For example, policymakers need to know: (a) if consumers are aware of the risks associated with using the product, (b) whether knowledge of how injuries occur affects the consumer's use behavior, and (c) if consumers consider safety a relevant dimension when selecting and using products.

CORRELATES OF CONSUMER SAFETY BEHAVIOR

Most of the original work on safety appears in the pyschology literature under the broad area of *accident proneness.* This term deals with the concept that certain people are more likely to have accidents than others. The reported findings, which normally deal with industrial accidents, are not consistent. One reason for this inconsistency is that accidents are, comparatively speaking, rare events, so it is difficult to get an accurate estimate of an individual's propensity for an injury. Often accident histories covering several years are required to estimate this propensity. Normally, analyses of these data are based on the assumption that the process generating the injury is stationary; consequently, intervening variables can easily confound the results. This lack of stationarity would seem to be especially true for injuries related to the use of consumer products, since product design and product usage may vary considerably over short periods of time.

To get around the need for an extended period of analysis and the assumption of stationarity, some researchers have looked at near-accidents or minor accidents. Guilford, in a laboratory kitchen experiment, observed the working patterns of 226 female subjects and classified particular actions into a number of minor accident categories [4]. She correlated the observed poor use behavior (i.e., "accidents") with a number of demographic variables and the subject's driving record. Significant intercorrelations were found between kitchen and automobile accident histories, thus supporting the

59

hypothesis that accident incidence in one environment has a positive relationship to accident incidence in other settings. Demographic variables were not found to be associated with "accident proneness."

Staelin and Weinstein looked at the reported use behavior of 187 adults [18]. Subjects were asked a battery of questions concerning how they behaved in specific types of situations such as pouring or handling volatile liquids and using rotary power mowers. Their responses were rated by safety experts with respect to the likelihood that a given behavior might lead to an injury; the scores were then aggregated over all questions, yielding a scalar measure, or index, of the individual's safe use behavior.

This reported safe use behavior index was cross-validated in two ways. The measure was found to be monotonically and statistically related to actual reported injuries within the household. For example, only 5 percent of the respondents who scored in the top quartile on the reported use behavior index indicated that someone in their household had a consumer product–related injury in the preceding two years, while the figure was 20 percent for respondents scoring in the lowest quartile. Second, a supplementary sample was asked not only how they behaved but also how they should behave for a number of situations. The correspondence between the responses to these two questions was positive but low (correlations ranging from .3 to .6), suggesting that respondents tended to report their actual behavior and not the behavior they felt might be appropriate. (It is important to note that this form of questioning shows that, at least for this group of respondents, consumers do not always use products in the way they think the products should be used. This finding is significant when evaluating the efficacy of safety information, since it implies that just because a consumer feels he knows how to behave safely, one cannot assume that this consumer will use the product in the fashion perceived to be safe.)

The reported use behavior served as a dependent variable in a regression analysis. The independent variables included measures of the respondent's knowledge of safety principles and his or her aversion to general situations concerning risk. Knowledge was measured in two ways. First an "IQ test" of safety principles was given. Typical questions were: "Why can a bird sit on a high voltage wire

60

and not get electrocuted?" "How do pot holders protect you from being burned?" and "What keeps a step ladder from tipping over?" Also, each subject was asked a series of self-reporting questions concerning his or her ability to explain how consumer products work. Risk aversion was measured by asking the subjects to determine the monetary or time value associated with avoiding specific risks. Some of these questions concerned hypothetical situations (e.g., auto racing), and others were actual behavior (e.g., properly filing income tax returns). The results indicated that safe use behavior is positively associated with knowledge of how products work and knowledge of the safety principles, and is negatively associated with the propensity to take risks. The authors interpreted the first two findings to imply that safer behavior is positively associated with increased knowledge of *why* one should behave safely, that is, the causes and potential hazards (risks) of specific products. Due to the cross-section nature of the data, they could not infer from the above results that more consumer safety information will lead to safer behavior.

A second study involving use behavior and its relationship to knowledge was conducted using 500 high school juniors in three Pittsburgh schools. Thirty-five classrooms of these students were randomly assigned into either an experimental or a control group. Both groups were given a pretest, and then the experimental group received eight 35-minute lectures on the principles of product safety. These lectures, given over a ten-week period, concerned such principles as grounding, heat transfer, the concept of protection from the energy source, and characteristics of materials and fasteners. Then both groups were given a posttest.

The posttest, which was identical to the pretest, used a paper-and-pencil instrument aimed at assessing the student's (a) knowledge of safety principles, (b) reported use behavior (similar to that reported in Sheth and Mammana [15]), and (c) perception of how he or she should behave (i.e., normative behavior).

The methodology used to compare the two paper-and-pencil measures was reported originally by Staelin [17]. It relies on a causal model that postulates that the educational program increases the student's knowledge of safety principles and that changes in this knowledge are associated with increases in normative behavior (i.e., knowledge of how one should behave in given situations to decrease the likelihood of an injury). The causal model was found to hold across all the schools tested even after controlling for grades, risk aversion, and previous exposure to specific courses such as physics, chemistry, and the like. However, the causal link did not extend to changes in use behavior (i.e., students who demonstrated an increase in knowledge of normative behavior did not report that they altered their use behavior during the ten-week experimental period). There are at least two plausible explanations for this latter finding. First, the educational program had no influence on behavior. Second, the time between tests was insufficient to measure changes in behavior, since many of the use situations tested were not encountered by the student during the test period. Consequently, the student was precluded from altering his behavior.

In summary, it appears that by increasing a consumer's knowledge of how products work and his understanding of the principles that affect the safety of a product, we can also increase his awareness of how to use these products safely. The evidence on actual changes in behavior is less conclusive, although there is a definite positive association between increased knowledge and safer use behavior. Thus, we still do not have an accurate measure of the benefits of consumer education. The costs of setting up an educational program dealing with product safety are comparatively small compared to those required to establish a regulatory agency. Yet, there is also the implied cost of displacing another subject if instruction were to be given in the typical high school program which has a fixed program capacity. The least expensive approach might well be to have a government agency provide educational material in readable pamphlet form.

RISK AND INJURY

As mentioned earlier, another factor highly associated with use behavior is the consumer's propensity for risk. Many consumer products are inherently risky (i.e., there is some probability of having an injury); thus, whenever a consumer uses one of these products he or she is forced to make a trade-off between the probability of incurring an injury and the cost associated with using the product in a safer fashion. Some of these latter costs may be in terms of time, that is, working more carefully, driving slower, using safety devices such as seat belts, reading the instructions, and so on. Others involve a one-time cost of paying more money for a safer design. In any case, on the basis of their awareness and understanding, consumers select a desired level of risk that balances these costs with the probability of injury. The question then becomes: What happens when the product design is altered so that the product is inherently safer? For example, what happens if a tractor is designed to have a wider wheel base, thus increasing the stability of the vehicle on hilly terrain?

One might conjecture that given a safer product, consumers will not alter their use of the product, so the new design will result in fewer injuries. However, there is no guarantee that consumers will not alter their use behavior. In particular, since the overall risk level is now lower the consumer may decide to reduce his "costs" (in terms of using the product safely)—which could maintain the original risk level or even increase it. With respect to our tractor example, consumers may ride the safer tractors on steeper hills so that they can farm more land. Similarly, consumers may ignore reading instructions because they preceive that product standards are such that the risk of injury is insignificant.

This concept of altering behavior as a consequence of changing levels of risk was investigated by Peltzman for automobiles [13]. He maintains that the 1968 auto safety regulation has decreased the risk of death from an accident more than an unregulated market would have, but that drivers have offset this decrease by taking greater risks. To support this contention, he showed that there has been an increase in both property damage and the total number of automobile accidents since the inception of the safety standards, and that the incidence of accidents has shifted somewhat from drivers to pedestrians.

The above reasoning rests heavily on a specific conceptual model of consumer behavior: namely, that the consumer first notices the design change and the resultant change in safety level, and then explicitly makes a trade-off between probability of injury and cost of behaving safely. There is little evidence to support this model other than that provided by Peltzman. However, researchers have noted increased search activity when the consumer perceives the purchase to be risky [2]. Researchers should be encouraged to learn more about the viability of the concept of trade-offs between probability of injury and cost of behaving safely.

It is interesting to speculate how this hypothesized trade-off between risk and cost of safe use behavior can be adopted to design programs for reducing injuries. For example, Great Britain has successfully used (as measured by short-term increases in the use of seat belts) 30-second television spots that show people disfigured from automobile injuries. The message links the injuries with nonuse of seat belts. Perhaps the seat belt use-behavior change is due, not to changes in levels of knowledge concerning seat belts and their ability to save lives, but rather to the fact that the advertisements altered people's perceptions of the risks associated with an injury. This reasoning is particularly viable when one considers the empirically observed biases associated with human decision makers [16]. Thus, given the concrete example of a particular type of injury, the consumer anchors on this example to reestimate the probability of a severe injury. Consequently, the perceived risk of not using a seat belt is increased. Similar reasoning suggests that consumer education programs would be more successful if they were to dwell more on the possibilities of injuries occurring than on why they occur.

INFORMATION SEEKING

One of the major alternatives to standards and regulation is to provide the consumer with more and better safety information and then to rely on the free market system to influence manufacturers to produce safer products. Congress gave the CPSC ample powers to collect and disseminate safety information. Also, industry has adequate and accessible channels to provide this type of information. Finally, there are independent third parties who can provide safety information via seals of approval or other types of certification.

The empirical evidence on the influence of safety information in the purchase decision process is mixed. Parkinson conducted a laboratory-type experiment in which 198 adult females were asked to select one brand from among four unknown alternatives in four different product categories [12]. Three of the four brands had some sort of seal or certification; the fourth had none. The results indicated that in the absence of other informational cues such as known brands, differential prices, and physical dissimilarities, the presence of a familiar seal or certification is a positive brand-selection inducement. Also, seals were found to be the most credible source of information when compared to advertisements, salesmen, and friends. Yet, consumers demonstrated little knowledge about the actual meaning of the seals, attributing a great deal more importance to the presence of the seals than was justified by the existing seal-granting programs. This finding was consistent with the fact that the impact of a seal on an individual's perception of a product was almost independent of the identity of the seal for those that are commonly known.

Kuehl and Simon reported on a survey of over 2,000 households interviewed to determine their attitudes on product safety [8]. In general, consumers said they had a strong safety concern for products such as food, drugs, cosmetics, and toys. Yet, only 30 percent of the respondents when purchasing toys reported considering safety "a lot," while 52 percent considered it "a little." Similarly, only one-third said they were highly concerned about the safety of toys in particular. Thirteen percent felt that poor design was the single most important cause of accidents associated with toys, while 87 percent attributed the cause to misuse or failure to follow or read instructions. When asked how often they read directions, only 23 percent indicated they read them all or most of the time, and 46 percent did not read directions any of the time.

Similarly, Staelin and Weinstein reported that safety was rarely mentioned in unaided recall as a factor considered prior to purchasing consumer products [18]. The largest group of consumers (21 percent) to mention safety as a criterion used in the purchase decision were involved in purchasing power tools. However, when subjects were asked to rank the importance of six prespecified factors (price, special features, quality, brand name, safety, and the retail store), the results were much different. In this case, safety was felt to be the most important factor for expensive toys, second most important for power tools, third for inexpensive toys, and fifth for appliances (both large and small).

Why the difference between the two types of responses? Perhaps consumers do not consider safety to be a unique dimension and thus

65

are not likely to mention it specifically. Or they may feel that the government already requires that all products be safe, so they do not need to explicitly consider this dimension in choosing among products, even though the safety dimension carries significant weight in an absolute sense.

In seeking safety-related information, Staelin and Weinstein's respondents mentioned material supplied by the manufacturer as the source most used and most useful. Testing groups such as the Underwriters Laboratories and publications such as *Consumer Reports* were less likely to be used than, say, friends or advertisements. In fact, the only group of consumers who tended to use technical sources such as *Consumer Reports* for safety information were those with considerable education. Consumers who used industry-controlled sources such as advertising, product literature, and testing results tended to behave safer, to be more risk averse, to know more about the safety principles associated with consumer products, and to feel capable of explaining how consumer products work. In summary, industry-controlled sources seemed to be used most and were more likely to be used by consumers with safe use behavior.

A recent study reported by Pittle discusses the advertising agency's views on the wisdom of industry providing safety information through advertising [14]. Twenty-one of the 100 largest advertising agencies responded to a mail questionnaire. The majority of respondents indicated that they believed safety to be a troublesome or ineffective merchandiser. They generally expressed the belief that consumers, rather than being persuaded to buy a product because it claimed to be safer than competing products, would be alienated by the mention of safety. One agency advised against safety claims for legal reasons. They noted that the word *safe* used in advertising might imply a warranty and thus could lead to lawsuits. They pointed out that the National Advertising Review Board (the industry policing agency) has warned against explicit safety claims in advertisements. This feeling may have been reinforced by the Federal Trade Commission (FTC). In recent years, the FTC has prohibited safety claims that are not "fully and completely substantiated by competent scientific tests" [6]. For instance, in 1972 the FTC told Firestone Tire and Rubber Company that it could not use the advertising phrase *the safe tire* or any other words that imply that its tires are safer under all conditions. Firestone also was told that any hint of a safety claim in an ad must be accompanied by a list of conditions that affect tire safety, and any reference to tire safety or performance superiority must be supported by competent scientific tests whose results are available to the public [7].

SUMMARY

One thing is apparent after reviewing the above material: Although the magnitude of the problem is great, there are no clear solutions that do not have attendant difficulties. Even if design and performance standards can be upgraded, we can optimally expect no more than a 20 percent reduction of injuries. Moreover, the question has been raised whether for some product classes the cost of new standards might not outweigh the benefits; the answer depends on the value one places on avoiding a human fatality.

Providing a consumer with information does not appear to pay off well either. Safer behavior seems to be related to better understanding of safety principles and knowledge of how products work. There is little to indicate that consumers seek out much information concerning safety, but this is understandable if we assume that consumers do not perceive much difference in risk between different products within a product class. Most information used by consumers comes from industry-supplied sources such as as advertisements and manufacturers' booklets. Yet persons who design ad copy believe it is unwise to mention safety in the ad. This could be a shortsighted business decision, since government regulators may feel the need to require a design standard where the competitive forces of the marketplace have failed. In defense of industry, however, this reluctance could stem from the Federal Trade Commission's requirement that ads contain detailed information concerning any safety claims.

Even if there were no government regulations on safety advertising, it is not clear that safety is currently a salient dimension for consumers. Consumers indicate that safety features are rarely used as a reason for selecting a particular product. Many users further indicate that they do not take the time to read the information now provided by the manufacturer. They also tend to attribute too much meaning to sources of information such as seals and certifications. Education aimed at raising awareness and changing behavior may be a promising solution—but it also raises a big question mark.

Perhaps the major reason consumers do not use information as a means to reduce injuries revolves around the fact that humans are extremely limited problem solvers. They cannot accurately assess factors as complex as safety. Consequently, they either use less complex dimensions or, if they do consider safety, they tend to use easier to understand proxies such as seals of approval or recommendations of friends. If, in fact, consumers are unable to process safety information, perhaps the best solution would involve either: (a) providing the consumer with strategies on how to better evaluate the safety aspects of the product or the risk inherent in using that product, or (b) presenting the information in such a way as to reduce the cognitive skills required of the consumer. Clearly, the payoff could be great.

REFERENCES

1. Conley, Bryan C. "The Value of Human Life in the Demand for Safety," *American Economic Review*, 66 (No. 1, 1976), 45-55.

2. Cox, D. F. "The Sorting Rule Model of Consumer Product Evaluation Process," in D. F. Cox, ed., *Risk Taking and Information Handling in Consumer Behavior*. Cambridge, Mass.: Harvard Univ. Press, 1967.

3. Dick, Stan. "A Short Study of the Potential Effectiveness of Mandatory Standards," unpublished paper, Consumer Product Safety Commission, 1975.

4. Guilford, Joan. "Prediction of Accidents in a Standardized Home Environment," *Journal of Applied Psychology*, 57 (No. 3, 1973), 306-13.

5. Hays, J. R. "Human Data Processing Limits in Decision Making," in E. Bennett, ed., *Information System Science and Engineering, Proceedings*. First Congress on the Information System Sciences. New York: McGraw-Hill Book Co., 1964.

6. *In the Matter of Bridgestone Tire Company of America,* Federal Trade Commission File no. 752 3098 (May 15, 1975).

7. *In the Matter of Firestone Tire and Rubber Company, 81,* Federal Trade Commission, 398 (1972).

8. Kuehl, P. G. and M. E. Simon. "The FDA Listens: A Survey of Consumer Opinion," *FDA Consumer* (1973), 8-13.

9. Lave, Lester B. and W. Weber. "A Benefit-Cost Analysis of Auto Safety Features," *Applied Economics,* 2 (1970), 265-75.

10. Little, John D. C. "Models and Managers: The Concept of a Decision Calculus," *Management Science,* 16 (No. 8, 1970), B466-85.

11. Michaels, Robert J. and Roy J. Shanker. "Product Safety in Practice and Theory," paper presented at the 50th Annual Conference, Western Economic Association, San Diego, Calif., 1975.

12. Parkinson, Thomas L. "The Use of Seals of Approval in Consumer Decision-Making as a Function of Cognitive Needs and Style," in Mary Jane Schlinger, ed., *Advances in Consumer Research,* Vol. 2. Atlanta: Assn. for Consumer Research, 1975, 133-9.

13. Peltzman, Sam. "The Effects of Automobile Safety Regulation," *Journal of Political Economy,* 83 (No. 4, 1975), 677-725.

14. Pittle, R. David. "Advertising Product Safety," unpublished paper, 1975.

15. Sheth, Jagdish N. and Nicholas J. Mammana. "Recent Failures in Consumer Protection," *California Management Review,* 16 (No. 3, 1974), 64-72.

16. Slovic, Paul. "From Shakespeare to Simon: Speculations and Some Evidence About Man's Ability to Process Information," *Oregon Research Institute Monograph,* 12 (Apr. 1972), 1-56.

17. Staelin, Richard. "The Effects of Consumer Education on Consumer Product Safety Behavior," in William Perreault, ed., *Advances in Consumer Research,* Vol. IV. Atlanta: Assn. for Consumer Research, 1977, 380-7.

18. _____ and Alan G. Weinstein. "Correlates of Consumer Safety Behavior," in Scott Ward and Peter Wright, eds., *Advances in Consumer Research,* Vol. 1. Urbana, Ill.: Assn. for Consumer Research, 1973, 88-100.

19. Tokuhata, George. "Childhood Injuries Caused by Consumer Products," unpublished paper, Pennsylvania Department of Health, Division of Research and Biostatistics, 1972.

20. U. S., House of Representatives. *Hearings on H.R. 8110, H.R. 8157, H.R. 260, and H.R. 3813 before the Subcommittee on Commerce and Finance of the House Committee on Interstate and Foreign Commerce,* 92nd Cong., 1st and 2nd sess., P.T. 3, at 1135 (1971-2).

COMPLIANCE WITH PRODUCT RECALL REGULATIONS: THE SMALL BUSINESS PERSPECTIVE

Mary C. Harrison
Louisiana State University

This study examines compliance with product recall regulations among small food processors. The author found that small food processors are not as well prepared to conduct product recall as their larger counterparts. She then recommends steps that these firms can take to improve their product recall preparedness.

One of the key issues in the consumer movement that developed during the 1960s was product safety. The question was often asked whether consumers were being adequately protected against unreasonable risk of injury from hazardous products. Consumer advocates were quick to expose faulty automobile design, adulterated food products, and hazardous emission of radiation from color television sets. The documentation of the existence of such hazardous products played a crucial role in the passage of significant product safety legislation.

This legislation provided a variety of enforcement tools that federal agencies could use to ensure compliance with the law. The Consumer Product Safety Act of 1972, for example, granted the necessary authority to the newly established Consumer Product Safety Commission (CPSC) to require a manufacturer to recall, repair, refund, or replace a defective product [6]. The Motor Vehicle Safety Act of 1966 requires manufacturers of motor vehicles to notify, by certified mail, all dealers and first purchasers of any safety defect the companies discover [3]. Although this act does not specifically designate product recalls as an enforcement procedure, over 43 million vehicles have been recalled since the act was passed [8]. The Food and Drug Administration also uses the product recall as its primary enforcement procedure, even though no statutory authorization exists for such action [1, 7].[1]

NATURE OF THE STUDY

The purpose of this study was to examine the small business perspective regarding compliance with product recall regulations in one particular industry: food. This industry was selected on the basis of its large number of firms, many of which are small, and its complex distribution channels, which make it difficult to locate purchasers of the recalled product. By comparison, the automobile, tire, and television industries are composed of a small number of large firms that use short distribution channels and that often record the names and addresses of purchasers.

Primary data were collected from food processors located in Texas to determine their product recall organization and procedures and to assess their capability of conducting a recall efficiently. Three hundred sixteen food processors were selected for a mail survey from a random sample, stratified by size and food product type, from the *Directory of Texas Manufacturers.* It was not known at the time of the selection whether any of these firms had conducted a product recall. Information regarding the nature of the recall, procedures implemented, and the impact of the recall on the firm was requested from those reporting recall experience. In addition, personal interviews were conducted with 20 Texas food processors to acquire further insights into their recall procedures and problems. The food processors were selected on a judgment basis, with primary emphasis on having product recall experience. An attempt was made to include firms of all sizes, geographically distributed throughout the state, and producing various types of food products.

Personal interviews were also conducted with enforcement and compliance officials of the Food and Drug Administration's Dallas office. Information was obtained concerning the agency's regulations

---

[1]The Federal Food, Drug, and Cosmetic Act of 1938 provides only for the enforcement procedures of seizure, injunction, and prosecution.

for firms conducting product recalls and the agency's procedures for monitoring the recall activities of these firms.

RESULTS

Of the 316 questionnaires mailed to food processors, 106 (33.5 percent) usable responses were returned. The chi-square goodness of fit test showed that the proportion of firms in each size and product type category in the original population was not statistically different from that of the 106 respondents.

Marketing Organization

Types of food produced. Table 1 shows the types of food produced by, as well as the sizes of, the firms surveyed. The type of food product processed by the firm affects the likelihood that the firm will have to recall a product representing a serious health hazard. Some types of products are more subject to adulteration or bacterial contamination than others due to their physical nature or their method of packaging. Bakery products, for example, might become stale or moldy, but they would not cause serious health injury. Canned vegetables, however, are subject to the growth of deadly bacteria, such as botulin toxin, when canned improperly.

Geographic distribution of products. Smaller firms are more apt to limit the geographic distribution of their products to their local area or state than are larger firms (Table 2). It is generally easier and less costly to remove a product from its distribution channels in a limited geographic area. When the area of distribution is large, the firm may have to delegate more of the responsibility for tracing the product and disposing of it to members of its distribution channels. Also, the expense of transporting the product back to the plant will be greater.

The concentration of small firms in intrastate distribution has traditionally meant that many of them are not under the direct jurisdiction of the Food and Drug Administration or the Department of Agriculture. Currently, there is a trend toward federal jurisdiction over food processors involved in intrastate commerce. The Whole-

TABLE 1

TYPES OF FOOD PRODUCTS PROCESSED, BY FIRM SIZE

Types of Food Products[a]	25 Employees	25–99 Employees	100 or More Employees	Total
Meat, poultry, fish	15	12	5	32
Fruits, vegetables, juices, canned specialties	3	5	8	16
Flour, grains, cereals, bakery products	9	6	2	17
Oils & shortening	2	2	5	9
Dairy products	4	9	4	17
Soft drinks, carbonated water	4	3	4	11
Candy & confectionery products	3	1	0	4
TOTAL	40	38	28	106

[a]Although 15 of the responding firms indicated that they supplied products from more than one product category, the firms are shown here in the category from which they were originally selected.

TABLE 2

GEOGRAPHICAL DISTRIBUTION OF PRODUCTS, BY FIRM SIZE

Geographical Distribution	25 Employees	25–99 Employees	100 or More Employees	Total
Intrastate	27	17	8	52
Interstate	13	21	20	54
TOTAL	40	38	28	106

some Meat Products Act and the Wholesome Poultry Products Act, passed during the 1960s, permit the Department of Agriculture to assume jurisdiction over meat and poultry processors operating solely within their own state if the department determines that the state health authorities are negligent in acting against firms producing adulterated meat and poultry products. These processors remain under the department's jurisdiction until it is determined that the state authorities will enforce regulations at least equal to federal regulations [4, 5]. Also, many state health authorities request assistance from the FDA during recalls limited to their states. Lack of funding has forced many state health authorities to operate with inadequate laboratories and manpower.

Structure of distribution channels. The smaller food processors use approximately the same distribution channels as larger firms (Table 3). The only important difference found here was in regard to the eight small firms, mostly bakeries, that primarily distributed from processor directly to the consumer. Half of the firms indicated that they also sold to institutions and other food processors. The firm's distribution channel structure affects the complexity of the product recall process. Firms that use many types of middlemen, that sell to institutions or other food processors, or that distribute

TABLE 3

PRIMARY DISTRIBUTION CHANNEL USED,
BY FIRM SIZE

Channel Structure	25 Employees	25–99 Employees	100 or More Employees	Total
P-B-W-R-C[a]	10	13	13	36
P-B-R-C	2	2	1	5
P-W-R-C	9	9	6	24
P-R-C	11	14	8	33
P-C	8	0	0	8
TOTAL	40	38	28	106

[a]P = processor, B = broker, W = wholesaler, R = retailer, C = consumer.

75

TABLE 4

PERSON RESPONSIBLE FOR RECALL ACTIVITIES
BY FIRM SIZE

Position of Person	25 Employees	25–99 Employees	100 or More Employees	Total
President or owner	31	28	12	71
Plant manager	8	8	10	26
Director of marketing	1	2	4	7
Quality control manager	0	0	2	2
TOTAL	40	38	28	106

products under a private label must notify and coordinate their recall activities with many customers.

Recall Preparedness

The person responsible for major policy decisions in the event of a recall is usually the firm's president or owner, regardless of the firm's size (Table 4). The plant manager is sometimes given this responsibility, particularly in multiplant firms. In a few of the larger firms, the marketing director or quality control manager was reported as having this responsibility.

Knowledge of FDA regulations. Smaller firms are less apt to have an individual in the firm who is knowledgeable about Food and Drug Administration regulations for product recalls (Table 5). This may reflect a perception on the part of many small processors that knowledge of federal regulations is unnecessary because they only distribute intrastate. It may also reflect a less specialized management capability due to financial constraints. In either case, the lack of familiarity with FDA procedures may prolong the decision-making process and the recall itself.

TABLE 5

KNOWLEDGE OF FDA RECALL REGULATIONS, BY FIRM SIZE

Firm Size	Number With Knowledge	Number Without Knowledge	Total
25 employees	10	30	40
25–99 employees	15	23	38
100 or more employees	16	12	28
TOTAL	41	65	106

$\chi^2 = 6.328$, significant at .05 level.

TABLE 6

PROCESSORS WITH WRITTEN RECALL PROCEDURES, BY FIRM SIZE

Firm Size	Number With Procedures	Number Without Procedures	Total
25 employees	4	36	40
25–99 employees	5	33	38
100 or more employees	13	15	28
TOTAL	22	84	106

$\chi^2 = 15.51$, significant at .005 level.

Existence of written recall procedures. Smaller firms are also less likely to have written product recall procedures (Table 6). Only 21 percent of the respondents indicated that their firms had written recall procedures, and these firms were predominately large. A firm that has adopted a basic recall program before a recall occurs has a decided advantage, since many of the initial decisions and assignments of responsibility have been made. It is reasonable to expect that a firm with written recall guidelines will be able to minimize the costs and time involved in conducting a product recall.

Use of identification coding. Small food processors may encounter greater difficulty in locating recalled products because they are less likely to place identification coding on their packaging (Table 7). If the recall were necessitated by a production error, the code would serve to isolate the time period in which the error occurred. When coding is not used, the firm must remove all units of the suspect product from its distribution channels.

The most commonly used type of coding, regardless of the size of the firm, is the production date of the product (Table 8). Some of the larger firms reported changing lot or batch numbers with every

TABLE 7

PROCESSORS WITH IDENTIFICATION CODING ON PACKAGING, BY FIRM SIZE

Firm Size	Number With Coding	Number Without Coding	Total
25 employees	19	21	40
25–99 employees	32	6	38
100 or more employees	28	0	28
TOTAL	79	27	106

χ^2 = 19.85, significant at .005 level.

TABLE 8

TYPES OF CODING ON PACKAGING, BY FIRM SIZE

Firm Size	Lot or Batch	Production Date	Expiration Date	Total
25 employees	4	15	4	23
25–99 employees	13	21	13	47
100 or more employees	11	25	8	44
TOTAL	28	61	25	114[a]

[a]Multiple responses were received from 45 of the 79 firms using coding.

work shift change to provide an even shorter time period than is possible with a production date. Firms producing highly perishable products often used a product expiration date for easy rotation and removal from the retailer's shelves. The small firms coding their packages tended to use only one type of coding, whereas large firms were more apt to use multiple coding methods.

Use of shipping records. Of the firms using identification coding on packaging, small firms are not as likely to maintain shipping record systems that identify individual customers (Table 9). Maintenance of such records enables the firm to contact only those customers who actually received the suspect product units. Such record-keeping systems should help the firm trace the product quickly and efficiently. Larger processors also appear to maintain these records longer than smaller firms (Table 10). The difference may be due to a longer average product life, since that is the crucial factor in determining the length of time records are kept.

The maintenance of shipping records may represent a tedious and costly task for the small food processor without computerized operations. Firms distributing only in their local area, for example, may determine that the cost of the system outweighs the benefits. In the event of a recall, these firms may prefer to check all customers' facilities for the suspect product units.

TABLE 9

PROCESSOR WITH SHIPPING IDENTIFICATION RECORDS, BY FIRM SIZE

Firm Size	Number With Records	Number Without Records	Total
25 employees	5	14	19
25–99 employees	16	16	32
100 or more employees	20	8	28
TOTAL	41	38	79

$\chi^2 = 9.371$, significant at .01 level.

Experience in public relations. The person responsible for public relations activities during a recall is usually the president or owner, regardless of firm size (Table 11). The plant manager sometimes has the responsibility, particularly in multiplant firms. Larger firms with more specialized personnel often delegate this responsibility to the public relations manager or the marketing director.

The individual responsible for these activities in the smaller firm is less likely to have previous public relations or advertising experience (Table 12). Although a higher percentage of the individuals in small firms had managed advertising campaigns, these individuals

TABLE 10

LENGTH OF TIME SHIPPING RECORDS KEPT,
BY FIRM SIZE

Firm Size	1–6 Months	7–12 Months	More Than One Year	Total
25 employees	3	1	1	5
25–99 employees	3	3	10	16
100 or more employees	6	1	13	20
TOTAL	12	5	24	41

TABLE 11

PERSON RESPONSIBLE FOR PUBLIC RELATIONS
DURING RECALL, BY FIRM SIZE

Position of Person	25 Employees	25–99 Employees	100 or More Employees	Total
President or owner	33	31	13	77
Plant manager	5	2	8	15
Public relations manager	1	3	4	8
Director of marketing	1	2	3	6
TOTAL	40	38	28	106

TABLE 12

PUBLIC RELATIONS EXPERIENCE OF PERSON RESPONSIBLE FOR THIS ACTIVITY DURING RECALL, BY FIRM SIZE

Firm Size	Number With Experience	Number Without Experience	Total
25 employees	13	27	40
25–99 employees	22	16	38
100 or more employees	22	6	28
TOTAL	57	49	106

$\chi^2 = 14.47$, significant at .001 level.

were less likely to have the more relevant experience of writing press releases and conducting press conferences. Previous public relations experience should help prepare the individual to handle the press during an awkward, and often embarrassing, time for the company.

Impact of Recall

The product recall's impact on the firm was analyzed for the 27 firms reporting such experience. The 27 firms included 13 food processors from the mail survey sample (12.3 percent of responding firms) and 14 from the personal interview sample. This analysis was largely qualitative due to the combining of samples and the small total number of firms with recall experience.

The food processors with recall experience included firms of all sizes producing various types of food products (Table 13). In general, the firms were similar to the mail survey sample in regard to geographic distribution of products, distribution channel structure, and the person responsible for major policy decisions during the recall.

81

TABLE 13

TYPES OF FOOD PRODUCTS RECALLED, BY FIRM SIZE

Types of Food Products	25 Employees	25–99 Employees	100 or More Employees	Total
Meat, poultry, fish	1	2	2	5
Fruits, vegetables, juices, canned specialties	1	2	3	6
Flour, grains, cereals, bakery products	2	2	1	5
Oils & shortening	1	1	1	3
Dairy products	1	1	1	3
Soft drinks, carbonated water	1	1	1	3
Candy & confectionery products	0	1	1	2
TOTAL	7	10	10	27

Effect on recall preparedness. As might be expected, the firms' levels of recall preparedness increased after they conducted their product recalls (Table 14). A comparison of recall preparedness before and after the firm's recalls revealed improvements in the following areas: (1) knowledge of Food and Drug Administration recall regulations, (2) existence of written product recall procedures, (3) adoption of identification coding on packaging, (4) maintenance of shipping records, and (5) public relations experience of the person responsible for this activity during a recall. The increase in the number of firms reporting knowledge of FDA regulations and public relations experience may simply reflect learning acquired during the recall. The remaining areas, however, are more likely to be the result of the firm's recognition of the importance of recall preparedness. It appears that a conscious effort was made to develop written recall procedures and to implement coding and record systems.

Evaluation of recall effectiveness. The firms surveyed generally gave a high rating to the effectiveness of their firm's recall activities

TABLE 14

RECALL PREPAREDNESS, BY FIRM SIZE

Recall Preparedness	25 Employees	25–99 Employees	100 or More Employees	Total
Knowledge of FDA regulations				
Before recall	2	4	6	12
After recall	5	9	10	24
Written recall procedures				
Before recall	1	2	4	7
After recall	5	7	8	20
Identification coding				
Before recall	2	7	10	19
After recall	4	8	10	22
Shipping records				
Before recall	2	4	6	12
After recall	4	5	6	15
Public relations experience				
Before recall	4	6	10	20
After recall	6	8	10	24

(Table 15). This may be attributed to the likelihood that only those firms that conducted a recall fairly effectively were willing to participate in the survey. A discussion of some specific problems encountered by the firms follows.

The firms that indicated some difficulty in locating the recalled products did not use coding or shipping record systems. The one exception to this was a firm that discovered an error in its coding which necessitated the removal of its entire inventory of that product from the 20-state area in which it was distributed.

The primary problem reported in obtaining customer cooperation was that the firms' wholesale and retail customers did not usually

TABLE 15

EVALUATION OF RECALL EFFECTIVENESS

Activities	Very Effective	Adequate	Inadequate	Total
Tracing recall products	19	6	2	27
Obtaining customer cooperation	23	2	2	27
Managing public relations	22	3	2	27
Recall activities, overall	20	7	0	27

maintain coding procedures and shipment information. Although many of the food processors maintained such records, the tracing process was still time consuming and costly because their customers did not maintain similar information.

The firms that encountered problems in the public relations area did so either because they conducted recalls of products representing a serious health threat or because the individual responsible for this activity had little previous experience. Widely varying views were expressed regarding the manner in which this function should be handled. Some firms stressed the need for openness and honesty, in the belief that consumers would remain loyal if this attitude were adopted. Other firms issued one press release when the recall was initiated and then refused further comment on the subject. One firm, which was conducting an FDA recall due to rodent contamination of its products, refused to issue any press releases even though local television and newspaper reporters remained on its parking lot for two days.

Financial impact of recall. Most firms were unwilling to disclose specific cost data regarding their company's product recall. The responding firms did indicate, however, the relative importance of various costs encountered. Most firms reported that the recall had some, but not a significant, financial impact on the firm (Table 16). It is possible that firms suffering severe financial consequences either refused to participate in the survey or gave incorrect information. The responses of those firms that did provide information appear plausible for several reasons. First, most firms were able to resume production and distribution shortly after determining the problem

TABLE 16

FINANCIAL IMPACT OF RECALL ON FIRM

Costs to Firm	Significant Impact	Some Impact	Little or No Impact	Total
Recall, overall	4	18	5	27
Lost sales	3	18	6	27
Customer refunds and adjustments	1	10	16	27
Tracing products	1	7	19	27
Notifying and coordinating with customers	0	7	20	27
Transporting products	0	7	20	27
Quality control	0	5	22	27
Promotion budget	0	4	23	27

causing the recall. Second, only a few firms indicated difficulties in tracing the recalled products. Finally, only two firms had recalled products that represented serious health hazards.

One of the firms willing to disclose cost data reported sizable losses as a result of the product recall. Some of the firm's major wholesale and retail accounts discontinued selling the entire line of products. Other customers who retained the products often moved them to a less desirable shelf position. The estimated value of the lost accounts was $250,000 per year, for a total cost of lost sales of $750,000 for the three years since the recall. The firm's "out-of-pocket" costs for the recall were $150,000. When these figures are combined with the increased quality control and promotion expenditures necessitated by the recall, the firm's total cost of the recall was almost one million dollars—about the same as their annual sales volume prior to the recall.

None of the firms experienced the most severe repercussion possible: bankruptcy. Bon Vivant Soup Company of Newark, New Jersey, experienced this fate after its 1971 recall, brought on by a death caused by consuming one of the firm's contaminated products [2].

Many firms instituted more stringent quality control procedures after their product recalls. The cost of implementing these procedures, however, generally was not significant (see Table 16). Most of the firms using identification coding now retain samples from each lot or date throughout the expected life of the product. One canner initiated a policy of not shipping its products until seven days after production in order to test samples of the product during a one-week incubation period. Several firms also indicated that they had instituted more stringent acceptance procedures for incoming raw materials ingredients.

Several firms increased their promotional budgets after the recall. One firm reportedly tripled its advertising budget. Most of them adopted a more aggressive selling program toward their wholesale and retail customers. One firm provided its salesmen with brochures explaining the cause of the recall and the procedures subsequently instituted to prevent a similar occurrence. Concern for maintaining the good will of their customers was expressed by most of the firms surveyed.

CONCLUSIONS AND RECOMMENDATIONS

This study has analyzed the capability of food processors to conduct a product recall efficiently and the impact of a recall on those firms that have conducted one. Although the impact on the firms surveyed generally was not severe, the possibility of a significant financial loss does exist. For this reason, it is suggested that food processors attempt to minimize the impact of a potential recall through the adoption of preparedness measures.

One individual within the firm should be given the responsibility for assessing the firm's recall preparedness level and for coordinating the firm's activities during a recall action. Depending on the size of the firm, this individual, the Recall Coordinator, may be the owner-president of the firm, the manager, the director of marketing, or some other decision-making executive.

In evaluating the firm's recall preparedness, the Recall Coordinator should begin by becoming knowledgeable about the Food and Drug Administration's recall regulations and procedures. The coordinator should then determine what types of quality control procedures, identification coding, shipping record systems, and public relations experience are necessary for his firm to conduct a product recall efficiently. Cost-benefit analyses should be performed before the firm adopts any of these measures. Finally, the coordinator should develop written procedures for his firm to implement during a recall. The procedures should specify the activities to be undertaken, their sequence, and the individuals responsible for performing each activity.[2] The effectiveness of the procedures may be tested by conducting a trial run or mock recall.

Larger firms appear to be in a better position to develop and implement recall preparedness procedures because of their financial and human resources. Smaller firms should endeavor to develop these procedures within the constraints of their resources. They should encourage their trade associations to assist them by sponsoring seminars or publishing information on product recall prevention, problem detection, and recall procedures.

Food industry trade associations could also serve as a useful vehicle for disseminating food safety information to the public. The consumer should be educated about the nature of product recalls, how to recognize adulterated products, and subsequent actions to take.

The impact of product recalls on the consumer is important since it is his patronage on which the existence of the firm depends. It is the consumer who, ultimately, bears the cost of product recalls as well as the risk of injury. Food processors must take the initiative in preventing adulterated products from reaching the market or in removing them as quickly and efficiently as possible. If food processors do not take the initiative in these areas, it is likely that con-

---

[2]An example of these procedures may be found in the author's study entitled, "The Development of a Model Product Recall Program for Small Food Processors," *1975 Combined Proceedings.* Chicago: American Marketing Assn., 1976.

sumerists will continue to pressure Congress for more stringent federal regulation of the industry.

REFERENCES

1. Committee on Government Operations. *Recall Procedures of the Food and Drug Administration*. Washington, D.C.: U.S. Government Printing Office, 1971, 3.

2. "FDA Wants to Widen Its Watchdogging," *Business Week* (July 24, 1971), 19.

3. "Public Law 89-563," *U.S. Statutes at Large,* 80 (Washington, D. C., 1966), 718-30.

4. "Public Law 90-201," *U.S. Statutes at Large,* 81 (Washington, D.C., 1968), 584-601.

5. "Public Law 90-492," *U.S. Statutes at Large,* 82 (Washington, D.C., 1969), 791-808.

6. "Public Law 92-573," *U.S. Statutes at Large,* 86 (Washington, D.C., 1972), 1207-33.

7. "Revision of Procedures for Recall of Products from the Market," *Federal Register,* 36 (June 15, 1971), 11514.

8. Schneider, Lawrence R. "Product Safety Legislation, Old and New," *The Conference Board Record,* 11 (Apr. 1974), 35.

PART 3

Policy Issues in Gasoline Marketing

DIVESTITURE OF THE LARGE INTEGRATED PETROLEUM COMPANIES

Fred C. Allvine
Georgia Institute of Technology

Allvine reviews the vertically integrated structure of competition in the petroleum industry. He discusses the problems associated with that structure and recommends ways of changing the situation to make it more compatible with the public interest.

The large integrated petroleum companies have recently experienced the most severe attack on the way they operate since the Justice Department's breakup of the Standard Oil Trust in 1911. State antitrust suits have been filed against several of the large petroleum companies by Connecticut, New York, Florida, Kansas, and California. The Federal Trade Commission has filed a major structural suit against the eight largest petroleum companies. The Congressional Hearing Record on the petroleum industry in the 1970s numbers into the tens of thousands of pages. More than 100 bills have been introduced by U.S. congressmen to require some form of divestiture of the integrated petroleum companies. Consumer organizations, including Ralph Nader's groups and the Consumer Federation, have advocated changing the way petroleum companies operate. Even Paul Newman has gotten into the act with a $300,000 contribution to a lobbying group that supports breaking up the big petroleum companies.

For many persons both within and outside the petroleum industry, the subject of divestiture is confusing and complex. One of the purposes of this paper is to help clarify why so many people are out to break up the industry and how the surgery could be undertaken. The specific topics to be discussed include:

- The structure of the petroleum industry
- Old and new complaints about the major petroleum companies
- Major proposals for physically breaking up the vertically integrated petroleum companies
- Major proposals for altering the conduct of the vertically integrated petroleum companies

COMPETITIVE STRUCTURE

Before considering the sources of pressure for divestiture and the various proposals made to accomplish this purpose, we must first understand the nature of competition in the petroleum industry. The petroleum industry is dominated by large integrated companies. There are eighteen companies that the Federal Trade Commission has categorized as the major integrated petroleum companies. They include Exxon, Texaco, Gulf, Mobil, Standard of California, Shell, American, ARCO, Phillips, Standard of Ohio, Getty, Shelly, Union, Sun, Marathon, Continental, Cities Service, and Amerada Hess [6]. All of these firms are heavily integrated from production through marketing, as can be observed in Table 1. The nature of their operations and their integration make these petroleum companies huge firms in American industry. For example, 5 petroleum companies rank among the 10 largest and 9 rank among the top 20 U.S. companies (assets and sales) according to the Fortune 500 survey.

The large integrated petroleum companies dominate each level of activity in the industry vis-à-vis the independents. As can be observed from Table 2, the 20-firm concentration ratio is 94% for domestic oil reserves, 70% for domestic oil production, 85% for refining capacity, and 79% for U.S. gasoline marketing. Seventeen of the largest integrated petroleum companies are among the top 20 firms holding reserves, producing oil, and having refining capacity. Fifteen of the 18 integrated companies are among the 20 largest gasoline marketers.

Closely associated with the integrated petroleum companies are the independent producers, estimated to number between 10,000 and 20,000. Historically, independents have drilled most of the exploratory wells. While some independents drill wildcat wells on their own leases, much of the drilling is done through farm-outs on

92

TABLE 1
PRIMARY TYPES OF COMPANIES IN THE PETROLEUM INDUSTRY AND OPERATIONS PERFORMED

Operation	18 Largest Integrated Petroleum Companies	Independent Producers	Major Brand Jobbers	Major Brand Dealers	Independent Refiners and Small Integrated Companies	Private Brand Marketers (Jobbers)
5. Marketing:						
Retail	O		O	X	O	X
Delivery	X		X		X	O
Wholesale	X		X		X	O
Storing	X		X		O	O
4. Pipelines	X					
3. Refineries	X				X	
2. Pipelines:						
Trunk	X				O	
Gathering	X				O	
1. Crude oil:						
Production	X	O			O	
Exploration	O	X			O	

X = Primary Activity, O = Secondary activity, ——— = Primary dependency relationship, – – – – = Secondary dependency relationship.

93

TABLE 2

CONCENTRATION RATIOS IN MAJOR PETROLEUM INDUSTRY ACTIVITIES

Companies	% Share of Domestic Reserves 1970	% Share of Domestic Oil Production 1969	% Share of U.S. Refining Capacity 1970	% Share of U.S. Gasoline Market 1970
Top 4	37.17	31.09	32.93	30.72
Top 8	63.88	50.54	58.07	55.01
Top 20	93.55	70.21	85.15	79.05
Number of 18 largest integrated petroleum companies in top 20	17	17	17	15

Source: *Preliminary FTC Staff Report on Its Investigations of the Petroleum Industry,* July 12, 1973, printed by the Permanent Subcommittee on Investigations of the Committee on Government Operations of the U.S. Senate, pp. 13, 14, 18, 22.

leases of the integrated companies. The major petroleum companies generally operate the higher-producing wells, while the independents control most of the smaller stripper wells—wells producing fifteen barrels per day or less. Independent producers sell most of their oil to the major petroleum companies' pipeline systems.[1]

At the downstream end of the industry, the integrated petroleum companies sell approximately 90 percent of their gasoline to major brand dealers and jobbers who do the final marketing. In the larger markets that account for a majority of gasoline marketing, the in-

---

[1]The FTC preliminary report of the petroleum industry found that almost 90 percent of independently produced crude oil was sold to the eighteen largest petroleum companies. See [6].

tegrated companies often do their own wholesaling and delivery. In this situation, the service stations are generally owned or controlled by the integrated companies and leased to major brand dealers. Jobbers carry out the wholesaling and service station development functions for the petroleum companies in most of the smaller markets. Through financial assistance and first-right-of-refusal clauses, the integrated oil companies also control a large number of jobber-owned stations.

Major brand gasoline marketing has several distinguishing characteristics. Specifically, it is basically a nonprice strategy built around brand image, intensive development of conveniently located stations, credit cards, and other types of sales promotion. The net result is that it is a high-cost method of marketing gasoline.

Independent refineries and smaller integrated companies selling private brand gasoline account for most of the remainder of petroleum industry activity. As Table 1 shows, the strength of these operations is in downstream (toward the final customer) activities. Most of the independent refineries own very little crude oil themselves and rely on the integrated companies and independent producers for their crude oil feedstock. The downstream taper of this segment of the petroleum industry is shown by the following estimates of the independents' 1970 market share in three key functions: (1) marketing—21 percent, (2) refining—15 percent, and (3) production—4 percent or less (estimate based on the crude oil self-sufficiency of larger independent refineries).

The independent refineries and smaller integrated companies normally sell private brand gasoline. There are hundreds of such brands and their names are not generally well known. Some of the most familiar private brands are: Sigmor, Hudson, Martin, Thrifty, Zephyr, Star, Merritt, Fill'em Fast, World, and U.S.A. Certified. Basically, private brand marketing is built on the philosophy of relatively high volume, low unit cost, and low price. With this marketing strategy, private branders have often sold their gasoline from two to five cents per gallon less than the major brands. Private brand operators are also distinguished by their emphasis on selling gasoline only, while the major brand stations normally sell tires, batteries, and accessories and do light service work on cars.

Unlike the majors, who control an estimated two-thirds of their own stations directly or through jobbers, the independent refineries and small integrated companies sell a majority of the gasoline they handle to independently owned, private brand gasoline marketers. Unlike the normal single unit, major brand lessee dealer, the private brand marketer is generally a chain operator who may have several hundred stations run by company employees. Similarly, the incidence of stations operated directly is higher for independent refineries than for the major petroleum companies. This is largely a result of the high-volume, low-price orientation of private brand marketing.

CHARGES AND COMPLAINTS

The outburst of hostility toward the large integrated petroleum companies is partially a result of lingering problems regarding how these companies operate and a whole set of new questions that raise further doubt about their performance. The first major category of problems deals with "old competitive complaints." There has been considerable friction within the major petroleum companies' own channels of distribution and marketing. Approximately 90 percent of major brand gasoline is sold through franchised dealers. Dealers and their association representatives frequently complain that the petroleum companies too tightly regulate the way they run their businesses and how they price their gasoline. The source of power over the dealers supposedly derives from the short-term lease and, in some instances, from company-operated stations. As a consequence of these practices, the dealer turnover rate is 25 percent to 30 percent a year—considered by many to be excessively high. The major brand jobbers, for their part, complain of being relegated to operating in the smaller markets and of being constrained by their suppliers from switching brands.

The primary competition to the major brand system is provided by the smaller independent refineries, with their private brand gasoline marketing outlets, and by the smaller integrated petroleum companies. Feelings run strong between the independents and the major petroleum companies. The independents complain that the large integrated petroleum companies subsidize their refining and marketing operations from their crude oil profits, and that this is an unfair method of competition.

Most of the complaints of customers and competitors of the major petroleum companies remained unresolved when the petroleum product shortages developed in 1972. At this time, a new set of problems appeared. Several of the major companies, including Phillips, Gulf, ARCO, and Sun, decided to withdraw from their less-successful marketing territories. As they did, their dealers and jobbers were left stranded, or could see that they eventually would be. In addition, some petroleum companies, such as Gulf, B.P., and Hess, converted stations, and often their best ones, from dealer to company operations. These developments created bitter feelings among many of those affected.

Panic swept through much of the independent segment of the petroleum industry as shortages became more acute. Private brand marketers and refineries found that product and crude oil originating from, or controlled by, the integrated companies were sharply reduced or completely terminated. The product and crude oil were reserved for the major brand system. Many of the independents were saved from disaster by the Mandatory Petroleum Allocation Act of 1973, but they still remember how close a scrape they had. Although the supply problems have eased, the independents find that they still are competing with the majors' subsidized marketing and refining operations.

Historically, the public has had little interest in the internal problems of the petroleum industry. The public did, however, start to become interested as they were affected by the heating oil shortages and gasoline shortages preceding the Arab embargo. Many questions were raised as to why the petroleum companies had not built adequate refining capacity to meet demand. While the companies placed much of the blame on government, other people recognized that the industry had a major influence on government policy.

The petroleum product shortage problem multiplied with the Arab Oil embargo of October 1973. Coming on the heals of the shortages were rapidly increasing petroleum product prices. Various government hearings and publications raised questions as to whether the petroleum industry might have cooperated with the Organization of

Petroleum Exporting Countries (OPEC) in quintupling the price of imported oil. Charges were also made that the petroleum companies were trying to take over coal and uranium industries at public expense. The uncovering of illegal political contributions in the U.S. and massive payoffs abroad further tarnished the industry's image. Finally, questions were raised whether, during a period of energy shortages and rising prices, Mobil should use funds to buy Montgomery Ward and Gulf should endeavor to purchase the Barnum and Bailey Circus. The net result was a rapidly growing anti-petroleum-company sentiment in the United States.

CHANGING STRUCTURE OF LARGE INTEGRATED PETROLEUM COMPANIES

The dissatisfaction from both *within* and *outside* the industry over the way the large integrated petroleum companies operate helps to explain why so many proposals for divestiture have been made recently. Major proposals for restructuring the large integrated petroleum companies are presented in Table 3. The attitudes expressed regarding the different propositions are based on my review of thousands of pages of recent hearings of the U.S. Senate and House subcommittees on vertical integration and divestiture, from research on two books I coauthored with James L. Patterson [1, 2] and from my testimony prepared for various subcommittees examining the petroleum industry.

The major piece of surgery proposed for the integrated petroleum companies was sponsored by Senators Birch Bayh and Philip Hart, respectively chairman and acting chairman of the Senate Antitrust Subcommittee. Their bill, S. 2387, would require that 22 of the largest integrated petroleum companies be *split into the four primary functions* of marketing, refining, pipelines, and crude oil. The Federal Trade Commission, in its suit against the eight largest integrated petroleum companies, has suggested that divestiture of pipelines and refining could well be a part of the remedy it would propose. By splitting the industry down the middle, the FTC is in essence also talking about a four-way breakup of the petroleum companies.

The logic behind the Hart-Bayh Bill and the proposed FTC remedy is that vertical integration is anticompetitive and contrary to public

98

TABLE 3

MAJOR DIVESTITURE PROPOSALS FOR ALTERING STRUCTURE OF INTEGRATED PETROLEUM COMPANIES

Proposal	Source of Support
1. Separate into *four* primary functions—marketing, refining, pipelines, and production	Congressional staff of Senate Antitrust Subcommittee and House Small Business Subcommittee. S. 2387, The Petroleum Industry Competition Act of 1975, sponsored by Senators Birch Bayh and Philip Hart. Also, FTC suit against eight largest companies could be settled by physical divestiture of several functions.
2. Separate into *three* functions—marketing and refining, pipelines, and production	S. 2761, sponsored by Senator John Tunney and approach supported by Senator Gary Hart. Compromise to four-way split, leaves similar operating functions together.
3. Separate marketing	Pushed by state and national major brand dealer organizations. Senate Bill 323, Dealer Day in Court, sponsored by Senator Frank Moss. Also, S. 739, sponsored by Senator Thomas McIntyre.
4. Separate pipelines	Congressional staff and S. 739 and S. 756, introduced by Senators Nelson and Abourezk.
5. Separate production	Supported by private brand marketers and introduced as amendment to the Emergency National Gas Bill.
6. Separate nonpetroleum energy operations	Congressional staff and amendment submitted by Senator Ted Kennedy to Emergency Natural Gas Bill and S. 489, sponsored by Senator Abourezk.
7. Separate OPEC operations	Anthony T. S. Sampson—writer and journalist, author of *The Seven Sisters*.
8. Nation-to-nation negotiation of OPEC prices	Proposed by Senator Henry Jackson and supported by several academics.

interest. However, my review of the petroleum industry's record over several years does not support a case against vertical integration in and of itself. The problem is that vertical integration permits the transmission of monopoly power at one level to other levels. To solve this problem, the monopolized functions should be identified and made competitive. Despite these abuses, vertical integration is often a very efficient means of organization and is widespread in U.S. industry. With regard to the petroleum industry, the public benefits from integration between the operating activities of refining and marketing. The valuable economies of scale and efficiencies that are achieved in this type of integration would be lost in a four-way split.

The second major proposal is a *three-way split* of the integrated petroleum companies, which is supported by Senators Gary Hart and John Tunney. Marketing and refining would be permitted to integrate to the extent dictated by the market, while pipelines and crude oil would be separated. The strength of this proposal is that it recognizes the beneficial characteristics of integration between refining and marketing and isolates the less competitive pipeline and crude oil activities. Yet, with regard to pipelines and crude oil operations, potential for monopoly power does not always lead to the actual use of that power. It must be recognized that regulation of the interstate pipelines by the Interstate Commerce Commission has kept monopoly abuses to a minimum. The ICC governs the rate of return on joint venture and independent pipelines. The regulated pipelines are required to operate as common carriers providing competitive access to all potential users. In addition, the Justice Department maintains a close watch over the big interstate joint venture pipelines, such as the Colonial, for signs of any anticompetitive activities. The published record of these pipelines does not appear to indicate that the interstate pipelines are much of a competitive problem. Some minor difficulties seem to exist in gaining access to and exit from pipelines, but these might well be solved by a consent decree rather than by divestiture of pipelines. Thus, effective methods are available to control conduct in a market rather than resort to the disruptive tendencies of divestiture.

Major brand dealers are the leading proponents of legislation at the national and state levels for *marketing divestiture*. They want to prohibit the major oil companies from directly operating stations and to slow down the revolutionary tidal wave approaching marketing that Dr. Patterson presented. Today, major brand marketing is at the stage of the neighborhood grocery store. The services provided are extremely expensive and, on a full-cost basis (including a competitive return on investment), range from twelve cents to sixteen cents per gallon [1, 3]. In contrast, the more efficient private brand method of marketing ranges from four cents to eight cents.

The perpetuation through legislation of the major brand dealer system will cost the public billions of dollars a year. In the public interest, there must be a major reduction in the approximately 200,000 service stations that exist today. Estimates from both within and outside the industry suggest that there are twice, or more, the number of service stations operating today than there would be if the marketplace were allowed to naturally weed out the inefficient and unnecessary stations. The overbuilding of service stations was an unfortunate legacy of the 1950s and 1960s. During the history of flush crude oil production, stations were built by the integrated petroleum companies to move crude oil and were not required to meet return-on-investment criteria for marketing. The consequence is that the U.S. has an extremely overblown service station system that makes little sense given current domestic crude oil shortages and high-priced foreign crude oil. Unfortunately, the major brand dealers are the ones suffering from the petroleum companies' bad judgment. To continue this overbuilt system is going to be extremely costly to the consumer. The proposals for marketing divestiture must be looked at as special-class legislation and not as legislation in the public interest.

Several bills have been introduced to *divest pipelines.* As previously argued, however, the advocates of such legislation are confused between potential monopoly power from the efficient joint-venture interstate pipelines and the abuse of that power. Pipelines may well be a significant problem intrastate, where there is no state common carrier law. This is a state problem, though, and needs to be dealt with at the state level.

With regard to joint-venture, interstate product pipelines, the competitiveness of these systems could be improved by requiring the pipeline companies to make available terminals for use by shippers who do not have their own facilities. This is often done by independent pipeline companies and would enhance competition within the joint-venture system. This change can, however, be accomplished without divestiture.

The fifth proposal is for *divestiture of crude oil operations* by the integrated petroleum companies. This proposal is supported by several of the downstream independent refineries, terminal operators, and marketers. It is based on the premise that the integrated companies, along with the independent producers, have administered high and noncompetitive prices for crude oil and have used integration to transmit this monopoly power all the way through to the marketplace. The independents also claim that the integrated petroleum companies have used crude oil profits to subsidize inefficient downstream operations [1, 2]. These actions retard the growth of independent refineries, terminal operators, and marketers, and they artificially maintain integrated companies' dominance over the industry. The public is also paying a higher price because of the inefficiency of the major brand system of marketing as discussed earlier.

The research carried out by Professor Patterson and myself supports the finding that the integrated companies have been able to manipulate the price of crude oil above the competitive level [7, pp. 200-1]. Very often the integrated oil companies earn little or nothing on their downstream investments, while crude oil is very profitable. Before the recent crude oil shortage, demand prorationing and the oil import program were used to support highly stable and noncompetitive crude oil prices. Now the OPEC oil cartel and the domestic oil shortages have eliminated the need for the older techniques to keep crude oil prices from falling to the competitive level.

If it were not for government regulations, the domestic price of oil would advance closer to the world cartel price set by OPEC. The accelerated squeeze on downstream activities would soon eliminate most of the independent refineries and other downstream operators [7, pp. 44-86]. This would not be a triumph of efficiency; rather, it would represent the use of vertical integration to extend the monopolized crude oil function to downstream activities of refining and marketing.

The challenge to this country is how to preserve a reasonably competitive and efficient petroleum industry and, at the same time, provide more incentive for finding oil. Higher oil prices are needed to encourage the search for and production of new oil, but this also increases the likelihood that profits will instead be used to further subsidize the integrated oil companies' downstream operations. One way to accomplish this goal is to enact the proposal for divestiture of crude oil operations by the integrated petroleum companies. Crude oil prices could be increased to stimulate the search for more oil without fear of further downstream subsidization. The downstream segments of the petroleum industry would be allowed to operate without subsidy and to reorganize more efficiently. The major societal savings would come from closing the large numbers of unneeded and costly-to-operate service stations. If gasoline marketing could be brought into the era of efficient mass merchandising, savings running into the billions of dollars could be effected.

In keeping with the anxiety over the operations of the large petroleum companies, Senators Kennedy and Abourezk have introduced legislation to *prohibit them from diversifying into other sources of energy*—basically into coal and atomic energy. The fear is that the huge petroleum companies will gain control of significant supplies of alternative forms of energy and then be able to increase prices above the competitive level. There is little evidence, or proof to date, that this has or will in fact happen in the future. A major fallacy of this proposal is that it is in a sense anticompetitive. It would eliminate a major source of competition in coal and uranium. Furthermore, it is in our long-run best interest to encourage energy development in the lowest-cost fields whichever they may be. Broad-based energy companies are in the best position to make this determination.

The federal government should be more concerned about how the petroleum companies enter new fields of energy. The government's antitrust division should investigate any mergers or purchases of the bigger coal companies by the large petroleum companies for any possible anticompetitive effect. However, prohibiting petroleum companies from entering new energy fields is far too simple a response to a complex issure. Proper energy diversification is beneficial in that the large petroleum companies may be able to take risks that others cannot. This seems to have been the situation with Gulf and Shell pouring hundreds of millions of dollars into the unsuccessful

103

venture of Atomic General to develop what was anticipated to be the more efficient high temperature gas nuclear reactor (HTGR).

The quintupling of OPEC oil prices over a two-year period, with prospects for further increases, has raised serious questions about the role of the international petroleum companies. Anthony Sampson, an editor of the *London Observer* and author of *The Seven Sisters,* believes that the interests of the Western world would be better served by *requiring the international oil companies to divest themselves of their OPEC operations* [4]. He bases his argument on the belief that the international oil companies carry out a worldwide prorationing system which holds the OPEC oil cartel together. While he may have assessed the problem correctly, his solution could be dangerous. Without the international oil companies' involvement in the Middle East, OPEC might well turn to the Soviet Union for assistance. Now we have oil, but the problem is the price. There is too much at risk for the Western countries to abandon the Middle East as Sampson suggests.

Senator Jackson has proposed one way around the problem inherent in Sampson's recommendation. Jackson would *take pricing responsibility for international oil away from the international oil companies.* In its place, there would be nation-to-nation negotiation of OPEC oil prices. It is obvious to those who have studied the developments in the Middle East that the international oil companies collapsed under OPEC pressure for exorbitant price increases. OPEC has been able to divide and conquer the oil companies, and each company is holding on to what little advantage it has in the world's largest oil fields.

The United States, as the world's largest importer of oil, has some leverage to help it negotiate a fair price for oil. The trouble is that the U.S. has not used any substantial muscle to bring down the world price of oil. Under Jackson's proposal, countries willing to sign irrevocable long-run contracts with reasonable prices and adjustments to increases in the wholesale price index would be guaranteed access to the U.S. market. If price negotiation with OPEC were taken away from the international oil companies, their continued involvement in the Middle Eastern oil fields should be of less concern to Sampson and others. Jackson's proposal for nation-to-nation negotiation of world oil prices seems worthy of further consideration.

REGULATION OF CONDUCT

Most of the attention in hearings, legislative proposals, and anti-trust activity has focused on changing the structure of the petroleum industry to alter performance. Another alternative is to require changes in *conduct* and leave the structure intact. The idea is to anesthetize the use of monopoly power so that it is not transferred by vertical integration to functions that would otherwise be highly competitive.

If properly conceived and implemented, changes in conduct should have results very similar to those obtained from restructuring the integrated petroleum companies. Prohibitions against certain types of conduct would also have the effect of encouraging the large petroleum companies to divest themselves of activities in which they are not efficient and do not possess expertise that gives them a competitive advantage. In line with this approach Mr. Jerry McAfee, chairman of Gulf Oil Company, has encouraged government policy that permits the industry to divest itself of unprofitable operations.

There are perhaps some advantages to legislation changing conduct instead of requiring divestiture. One important consideration is that the large petroleum companies would be less inclined to fight such legislation or regulation. This would be a way to avoid the long political and legal battle that would surely be involved in physical divestiture. Our experience with the Public Utility Holding Company Act shows how long and drawn out divestiture can be. Furthermore, the United States needs to proceed with solving its energy problems, and the battle over physical divestiture could delay energy development programs and might hobble the industry effort to raise badly needed capital.

Perhaps now is a "time for compromise" as proposed by Tom Sigler, vice-president of Continental Oil Company [5]. Most intro-spective petroleum company executives know that the petroleum industry has backed itself into some real problems with government. If the industry is allowed to surrender with dignity, then the battle with government can be called to a close and the articles of new conduct can be drawn and signed. If, however, the penalty for sur-render is too high, then the industry can be expected to fight on. It must be recognized that those who would prefer to "draw and quarter'' the large petroleum companies and make the event a public spectacle are not serving the best interests of the country.

Now with some argument made for prohibitions against certain conduct, the difficult task is to specify the changes to be implemented. Several of the practices of the integrated petroleum companies greatly restrict open market transactions involving crude oil and refined products. My research supports the conclusion of the 1973 FTC report regarding the adverse competitive impact of the exclusionary agreements among the large integrated petroleum companies. The summary paragraph of the 1973 FTC report on exclusionary practices reads as follows:

> In the many levels in which they interrelate, the majors demonstrate a clear preference for avoiding competition through mutual cooperation and the use of exclusionary practices. Together they dictate a common price for raw material and seek to stabilize price for refined product. Their common conduct with respect to pipelines and their tendency to bypass the market mechanism through the use of exchange and processing arrangements, has been clearly exclusionary. These exclusionary practices are directed at a common target—the independent sector of the industry. In sum, the majors continually engage in common courses of action for their common benefit. [6]

There are six important exclusionary practices employed by the major petroleum companies that may have to be changed or eliminated entirely to make the petroleum industry more competitive. First, refined product exchanges among the large petroleum companies keep a product from flowing into the open market where less-disciplined competitors would have a chance to make competitive purchases of supply. Second, difficulty in gaining access to and exit from the cooperative pipeline ventures results in constraining competition from smaller companies. This problem could be eliminated if the highly efficient, joint-owned common-carrier pipelines had terminal facilities for use by nonowners, as is the situation with the independent pipelines. Third, some petroleum companies have processing agreements for their crude oil that reduce open market sales of tight feedstock. Fourth, the integrated companies use crude oil pipelines to control most of the supply of independently pro-

106

duced crude oil. Independent producers should not be required to give up title to the crude oil that is transported in major owned and controlled pipelines. Fifth, crude oil exchanges, like product exchanges, make it difficult for those outside the tightly knit industry structure to gain access to supply. Finally, the joint bidding among the giant petroleum companies has worked to increase the bid price for exploration acreage and to reduce competition. The Department of Interior has already acted to reduce this problem by prohibiting the larger companies from bidding together.

The exclusionary practices have not been aired in discussions of the major oil companies regarding how conduct might be changed. However, no meaningful alteration of behavior can be expected without such legal requirements to break the ties that bind the large petroleum companies together.

Many proposals for reform coming from within the industry focus on dealer relations. Although this is not the most important problem, it is perhaps the most politically charged issue because there are approximately 150,000 major brand dealers. The petroleum companies' power over dealers could be sharply reduced by replacing one-year leases with long-term leases of three to five years, or "evergreen" contracts. Whatever the type of lease extension, termination could only result from significant infraction of fairly drawn dealer contracts. Continental, ARCO, and others seem to be in favor of such changes. With the new Dealer Day in Court legislation, however, they may have no choice but to give in.

Legislative proposals to restrict the petroleum companies regarding service stations can go too far. For example, dealer proposals and legislative bills have been introduced to prohibit direct station operation by petroleum companies (as the Maryland bill required). The petroleum companies should, however, be compelled to obtain mutual agreement with their dealers before converting from dealer to direct operations. Additionally, the petroleum companies should not be permitted to discriminate in favor of their direct operations.

To further free the dealer from control and undue influence from his landlord-supplier, the arbitrary "tank wagon" pricing system should be eliminated. Under the "tank wagon" system, petroleum companies grant temporary price reductions to their dealers with the intention that dealers will in turn reduce their prices. There are many problems with this system. The granting of price protection is inherently an arbitrary procedure that is subject to manipulation; it can be used to discipline noncooperative dealers. Price protection also has elements of vertical price fixing, which is per se illegal. Also, price protection results in cross-market subsidies which can have anticompetitive consequences. The "rack pricing" or "terminal pricing" approach proposed by Continental and used in experiments by Citgo and Phillips would ensure that all dealers were treated fairly. There would be a base price for gasoline that all gasoline dealers would pay to their suppliers. Fees could be charged dealers for use of the company's brand name, and a fair rental charge could be made for leasing service station facilities. Longer-term dealer leases and a rack-pricing system would make major brand dealers the independent business people they are supposed to be.

The last major area in which conduct of the large integrated petroleum companies must be altered involves the downstream independent refineries and marketing companies. Throughout most of the 1960s and 1970s, the downstream independents have been trying to compete against the crude oil–subsidized refining and marketing operations of the integrated petroleum companies. Without side payments there would be still fewer independent refineries in existence today. From the inception of the Mandatory Oil Import Program in 1959 through 1972, the smaller independent refineries received more than their proportionate share of valuable oil import tickets. This reduced the costs of crude oil to the smaller domestic refineries to a level nearer what competition would have set absent the oil import quota system and market demand prorationing. These two laws permitted the large integrated petroleum companies to regulate supply to support the administered, noncompetitive crude oil price.

Demand prorationing and the import quota system ended in 1972 and 1973 with the domestic shortage of oil and the regulation of the international crude oil market by OPEC. With the crude oil shortage, the domestic price of oil soared by nearly 150 percent from 1973 to 1975. Up went the profitability of crude oil, and down went integrated oil company earnings from refining and marketing to breakeven or loss levels. Were it not for the Mandatory Petroleum Allocation Act of 1973, which prohibited the majors from cutting off the independent refineries' supplies, and the crude oil entitlement program of 1975, which equalized crude oil prices, most independent refineries would be on the ropes today.

As a first step toward ending the practice of downstream subsidization, the integrated oil companies could be required to publish quarterly financial results by functional activities, as Gulf Oil Company recently did. The integrated oil companies have historically kept their functional operating results highly confidential. Disclosure of functional profitability could have some long-run salutary effects. Pressure would be exerted from a variety of sources to stop the practice of subsidization. Stockholders, recognizing that the loss operations are a drag on overall profitability, would pressure management to cease this practice. Independent refiners and marketers would certainly call attention to the anticompetitive consequences of the out-in-the-open subsidization. Finally, government policy-makers could question the need for higher crude oil prices when other activities were being subsidized out of crude oil profits.

Financial disclosure is now being advocated by Continental, Gulf, and Ashland. The Federal Energy Administration is contemplating compulsory disclosure of profitability by function. Senator Haskell's proposed Energy Information Act, S. 1864, would also require the collection and publication of data by function.

One question raised is: Does functional reporting go far enough? As a further alternative, the integrated companies could be required to make at least a marginal rate of return on refining and marketing or to divest themselves of these operations. For example, they could be required to earn at least one-half the overall corporate rate of return over a three- to five-year period. If unable to meet this minimum earning level, they would then be required to submit in six months a voluntary plan for divestiture of the function(s) they were unable to operate profitably and were subsidizing.

SUMMARY

This paper has reviewed the vertically integrated structure of competition in the petroleum industry. The industry is dominated by large integrated companies in all major functions, including exploration and production, crude oil pipelines, refining, product pipelines, and marketing.

An accumulation of complaints about the conduct and performance of the major petroleum companies has resulted in broad-based pressure to break up the petroleum industry. The problem with many of the proposals thus far is that they may not achieve the intended result. Effecting separation at the wrong level or making too many divisions could worsen rather than improve competitive performance.

Legislation or legal decision requiring changes in conduct is an alternative to the physical restructuring of the petroleum industry. Much the same end can be accomplished through changing conduct as by requiring physical divestiture. Legislation requiring changes in conduct merits further consideration.

REFERENCES

1. Allvine, Fred C. and James L. Patterson. *Competition, Ltd.: The Marketing of Gasoline.* Bloomington: Indiana Univ. Press, 1972.

2. _____ and _____. *Highway Robbery: An Analysis of the Gasoline Crisis.* Bloomington: Indiana Univ. Press, 1974.

3. "B. P. Pushing 'Low Service Units'; Still Emphasizing Jobber Outlets," *Oil Daily* (Jan. 21, 1976), 8.

4. Sampson, Anthony. "How the Oil Companies Help the Arabs to Keep Prices High," *New York Magazine,* 8 (Sept. 22, 1975), 48-55.

5. Sigler, Tom W. "Time for Compromise," speech delivered at the Indiana Oil Marketers Fall Convention, Sept. 17, 1975.

6. U.S., Senate, Committee on Government Operations, Permanent Subcommittee on Investigations. *Investigations of the Petroleum Industry.* Washington, D.C.: U.S. Government Printing Office, 1973, 5.

7. U.S., Senate, Committee on Interior and Insular Affairs. *Oil Price Decontrol.* Washington, D.C.: U.S. Government Printing Office, 1976.

CHANGES IN GASOLINE MARKETING: AN EVALUATION

James M. Patterson
Indiana University

Patterson argues that a marketing strategy based on a vertically integrated structure is ill-suited for the period that lies ahead for the oil industry. He examines the changes that have already begun to alter the nature of gasoline marketing and urges that new marketing strategies be developed.

The marketing strategy perfected by the gasoline industry in the late 1960s was in large measure a consequence of the peculiar structure of that industry. It was a strategy designed to generate product sales with only minimal attention to marketing profitability as such. Profits were lodged in tax-sheltered crude oil production, where with governmental support prices could be rigged and supplies controlled. Because all majors and most of the other important companies in the industry were, and are, vertically integrated, total system profit rather than profit at any functional level became the basis for strategy development.

To pursue a strategy of profit maximization at the marketing level which would restrict sales and hence tax-sheltered crude profits would clearly be suboptimal. Marketing (and refining) were clearly subservient to the need to produce and dispose of crude oil. It was, of course, desirable that marketing and refining be profitable, but it was not essential. For the tax-sheltered monopoly profits at crude to be realized, the crude had to flow. And for one's own crude to flow, it was necessary to gain control over downstream markets and to maximize the flow through one's own outlets. This is particularly true when most competitors are themselves vertically integrated.

The emphasis on the expensive, well-located, aesthetically appealing, supplier-controlled, dealer-operated, retail service station offer-

112

ing a single nationally advertised brand of gasoline, supported by a host of continuity promotions including gasoline credit cards (which was the normal way for major oil companies to market in the late 1960s), did not just happen. It reflected the logic of a vertically integrated structure with tax-sheltered monopoly profits at one functional level seeking both to protect and exploit that opportunity at other levels. In the case of the oil industry, it produced a top-heavy, expensive, and often inefficient marketing strategy that would not otherwise make sense.

Recently, however, a number of the factors that produced this strategy have begun to change. The result is that the oil industry has been left with a marketing strategy that is ill-suited for the period ahead.

The weakening of the crude oil profit center, more than anything else, represents *the* major change undermining the very foundation of the former marketing strategy. The old game plan of subsidizing downstream operations to move crude makes much less sense with the repeal of the percentage depletion allowance and the curbing of the expensive options. A dollar of pre-tax profit at the crude level is no longer worth several times the pre-tax profit dollar at other levels—at least in the United States. The foreign tax credit remains, but it was, and is, less influential on gasoline marketing strategy than the depletion allowance.

The end of oil colonialism and the rise in equity participation, along with increasing control of production by the exporting nations, means that the profits from greater foreign crude production no longer accrue primarily to the major oil companies. The largest share now goes to the host nation in the form of royalties and taxes and joint profits.[1] Also, control over the price of crude has shifted to the exporting nations.

Coincident with the shift in control over international crude production, domestic crude production peaked and began to decline after 1970. After May 1972, increments in volume had to be met with increased imports, and now the profit from imports is shared.

---

[1] Oil company share of the $11.40 price of foreign crude has been estimated at only 22¢.

113

None of this means that increased crude imports are profitless. Quite the contrary, the foreign tax credit is clearly one of the most valuable tax loopholes still around. Nevertheless, the relationships between crude volume and after-tax profit are more complex than before, and a marketing strategy designed primarily to generate volume with little regard for cost has ceased to be functional.

Not only have unbridled increases in crude consumption ceased to be the way to maximize profits for the integrated major oil companies, but they are even more undesirable from the standpoint of national policy. For a variety of political and economic reasons, conservation has become an important objective for all consuming nations. Aggressive marketing strategies, designed to encourage the growth of demand for petroleum products, would immediately be seen as counter to the national interest and would undoubtedly provoke immediate government sanctions.

There are many other more subtle changes that also challenge the continued viability of the old strategy. The experiences of the "shortage" have weakened brand preference and have made motorists more price conscious. There is a rising militancy among dealers who have had a taste of the good life, of high margins and short hours. Service has more or less taken a holiday, which has caused motorists to look elsewhere for car care. All of these factors and others are having a profound impact on the marketing of gasoline.

THE SEARCH FOR NEW STRATEGIES

The old strategy is bankrupt. It no longer reflects the realities of the last half of the 1970s. Where are profits to come from in a low-growth industry? Numerous projections see a 2 percent growth rate as about all that will be allowed.[2] Some additional profits will come from the gradual decontrol of regulated domestic crude and from increases in international crude prices that are now administered by OPEC. The oil companies have already had their big windfall profits from the massive price increases of 1973–74. Major future windfall

---

[2]*The Oil and Gas Journal* predicts gasoline demand will rise by 1.8 percent to 6.7 million gallons per day for 1976. This compares with the 2 percent increase of 1975 demand over 1974 [8].

gains are likely to be subject to confiscation. In any event, the price elasticity of demand and the deflationary impact on the world economy is beginning to make price increases less attractive—even for OPEC.[3]

With increases in consumption opposed by public policy, and with price increases meeting substantial resistance from customers and taxing authorities—both domestic and foreign—profit growth over the next decade must increasingly come from refining and marketing, that is, from more efficient operations. Some changes will take place in refining, but the major shifts will come in marketing. Marketing must now make money on its own. There is no longer any long-term justification for the subsidization of marketing by crude profits.

Many of these changes have already begun. Many more have been suppressed by the detailed regulation of the industry by the Federal Energy Administration. But as regulation subsides, and as pressure for profit growth mounts, changes will begin to emerge.

The most obvious change will be a radical decline in station population. The number has already fallen to less than 190,000 from the 1972 high of 226,000 branded outlets. Because market share was closely correlated with station share in any given geographic market, overbuilding was inevitable as long as marketing's role was to move the almighty crude.

The obvious consequence of this strategy was to reduce average station volume and hence to raise the retailing cost per gallon. The practice has its parallel in the parable called the tragedy of a commons [2]. In the parable, each herdsman knows that the benefit of adding an additional animal to a bounded commons accrues exclusively to him, while the negative effects of overgrazing are shared by all. As a consequence, each individual herdsman is compelled to

---

[3]During the first 11 months of 1975, OPEC's total petroleum production was down more than 12 percent from the previous year and equivalent to only about 70-75 percent of total production capacity. Saudi Arabia was down 21.2 percent from 1974, Kuwait by 30.2 percent, the UAE by 33.9 percent, Venezuela by 29.0 percent, and Libya by 87.1 percent [7].

115

add animals to the meadow even though the collective consequence of these individual decisions is ruin for all.

So long as gasoline marketing was subservient to crude sales, the ruin was postponed. Now that marketing must make money on its own, the day of reckoning has arrived. Low-volume stations are not only a drag on themselves, but they are also a drag on all other stations.

On the assumption that the average station will be doing 60 to 70 thousand gallons per month by 1980, the total number should decline to 160,000 by then. On balance, this decline should be seen as a good thing. In the first edition of *Theory in Marketing,* Richard Lundy asked in a classic essay: How many stations are too many? [4] That question is now being answered by signals from the marketplace rather than by directives from corporate headquarters. The result will be much lower retail costs as a consequence of higher average volume per station. Marketing gross margins will be more than halved, and economic efficiency will be improved.

On the negative side, the motorist will lose some locational convenience that the old system provided but made him pay for whether he wanted it or not. Also, as the total station population drops, and as those stations that remain increase in size, small-scale personalized retailing will disappear. For many motorists, this too will be a loss.

Related to the decline in station population will be a geographic concentration by brand of those that remain. The trend toward withdrawal from thinly represented markets was well underway before the embargo.[4] It will continue, but at a slower pace. As brand image declines in importance in the marketing picture, retail facility concentration will be less important, and scattered properties using secondary brands that can be economically supplied will be retained if they can achieve satisfactory volume as an off-brand with a price emphasis.

---

[4]Arco, American, Phillips, Gulf, Sun, and Continental all began plans for reconcentrations in 1972 (see [5]).

The end result of this trend will be fewer major brands in any given geographic market. It will have little or no impact on either competition or the range of choice available to the motorist.

One of the principal consequences of the significant increase in average station volume will be a rethinking of the way stations are operated. When gasoline retailing was treated as a break-even operation, the heavy reliance on lessee-dealers made sense for the majors. Now that is less clear. Many high-volume stations are just too profitable for dealer operations under the old tank-wagon pricing method. At 75 to 100 thousand gallons per month, the rewards to the dealer are way out of line with his contribution. Increasingly, these prime, high-volume stations, already owned by the supplier, will be converted to employee or agent operations. Several companies have already begun to move in this direction.[5]

In a direct sense, the motorist will probably gain from this trend. In an indirect sense, the impact is less clear. If employee operation increases the ability of the majors to focus price competition directly on offending price cutters, the chances for price competition are reduced. In this sense, the motorist may be the loser. This is an area of change that should be monitored to prevent lasting damage to the forces making for retail price competition.

The entire area of dealer management is in a state of change. Many suppliers are having trouble getting their dealers to be competitive. The growing militancy of dealers, coupled with the rise of "dealer rights" bills in Congress and the state legislatures, makes it harder to order the dealer around. Many dealers are staying open shorter hours and clinging to their newly won margins. Older methods of controlling dealer marketing practices and prices are either no longer appropriate or, as in the case of temporary tank-wagon reductions, too expensive to be used.

Again, the impact of these developments is mixed. The end of the "temporary competitive allowance" will strengthen intertype com-

---

[5]Gulf, which had 30,000 retail stations in 1970, had only 17,000 in 1976. In five years they plan to have only 14,000. Of these, they plan to have 20 percent company operated and 80 percent dealer operated [6].

petition and reduce the incidence of destructive price wars. On the other hand, without price support, the supplier will have much less influence over dealer prices. For those motorists addicted to major brands, the price will be higher on average. For those willing to use private brands, the average price will be lower, though there will be less variability.

Certain majors have been experimenting with incentive plans involving rent adjustments as a way of controlling lessee-dealer operations, but the big move is going to be into selective direct-employee operation of key, pace-setter stations in order to call the tune on the way the lessee-dealers operate and price in any given metropolitan market. With 25 to 50 key locations, an entire market can be regulated.[6] This becomes a feasible alternative to price supports and dealer controls.

Generally, this aspect of the trend to direct-employee operations must be seen as a positive development since it will increase the quality of service available to the motorist. This must, however, be balanced against the clear threat such operations pose to the vigor of intertype competition.

Coincidental with the rise in direct operations in profitable key locations will be a radical shift in the mix of retail operations. Specifically, there will be considerably less emphasis on traditional full-service operations, and much greater emphasis on fast-serve, less-service, and self-service operations. The profit potential of such operations has already been amply demonstrated by the pioneering private branders over the last decade and a half.

In the past, self-service was an offensive strategy designed to permit deeper discounts from major brand reference prices. In the future, it will be a defensive strategy, designed to reduce station payrolls and to get unit labor costs down. As a consequence, we can expect to see self-service become much more extensive.

---

[6]Dan Usner, of the Louisiana Retail Gasoline Dealers' Association, testified in his July 31, 1975, appearance before the House Judiciary Committee (Subcommittee on Monopolies and Commercial Law) that Exxon is able to regulate its dealers in New Orleans with 25 key direct operations.

By definition, the motorist will receive less service as a result of this trend. But he will now have a choice. In the past, he opted for full service because he had to pay for it whether he wanted it or not. Now he can have it if he wants to pay for it or he can opt for lower price. This should be seen as a positive development.

Tie-in operations with convenience stores, dairy stores, car-care centers, tire stores, car washes, and the like will also grow as new forms of retail synergy are sought to justify high-priced locations and quality management. This trend must also be regarded as positive. It represents a more diversified response to evolving preferences for different purchase combinations. One result of this trend will be to bring nongasoline retailers into the gasoline business. This too must be seen as a positive development, since these retailers are not committed to past practices and will introduce novel approaches to gasoline retailing.

One important consequence of all these trends is that the gasoline market is going to be much more segmented than has been true in the past. Furthermore, major brand suppliers can be expected to participate vigorously, and directly, in all of the segments. In the case of the minor majors, discounting under secondary brands will rise dramatically in importance. To some extent, this growth will preempt the role of the traditional independent marketer. More importantly, it will hasten the end of the old marketing strategy.

As the retail market begins to shift, so too will the ways of relating to that market. For example, we can expect the role of the traditional jobber to disappear in all important markets. Those that remain will become direct operators of branded chains of employee-run stations. Also, we can expect to see retail gasoline credit substantially curbed. It is much too expensive in a period when marketing margins are under severe pressure.[7]

The old dealer tank-wagon method of pricing is also an anachronism that is bound to fall. The bundling of brand franchise, credit, station rent, and product cost under one comprehensive price is no longer working well. Conoco has recently proposed that gasoline sales by refiners be separated from the sale of other commodities or

---

[7]Recent figures suggest that the cost of credit is 2¢ per gallon [5].

services and offered to any prospective buyer without franchise or lease requirements. Also, the sale of a brand franchise would be separated from the purchase of gasoline and the leasing of service stations [1].

Taken as a whole, these impending changes in the marketing of gasoline must be regarded in a favorable light. The homogeneous strategy of the past, which represented a massive economic waste and which failed to effectively recognize the real diversity of buyer preferences in the marketplace, is now giving way to a more stream-lined and diversified operation. This is good.

The one serious caveat is whether the residual price competition at retail will be sufficient to compel the sharing of the savings from more efficient operation with the motoring public, or whether these savings will be captured completely by the integrated retailer. If we are not careful, we will end up pumping our own gas and wiping our own glass without any significant reduction in marketing margins. This would represent a net loss from the consumer's viewpoint. Unless the present vertically integrated structure is altered, my guess is that convenience and service and marketing costs will be cut much more than marketing margins. In any event, the insistent pressures for increased marketing productivity are too strong to be resisted. The old strategy is doomed. New strategies are bound to emerge.

REFERENCES

1. "Broad Changes in Gasoline Marketing Practices are Proposed," *Wall Street Journal*, 88 (Sept. 18, 1975), 10.

2. Hardin, Garrett. *The Environmental Handbook.* New York: Ballantine Books, 1970, 36-7.

3. "If a Major Can't Make It in a Market," *National Petroleum News*, 64 (Feb. 1972), 43.

4. Lundy, Richard D., "How Many Service Stations Are 'Too Many'?", in Reavis Cox and Wroe Alderson, eds., *Theory in Marketing.* Chicago: Richard D. Irwin, 1950, 321.

5. *National Petroleum News*, 67 (Mar. 1975), 18.

6. *Oil Daily*, 26 (Dec. 17, 1975), 7.

7. *Oil Daily*, 27 (Feb. 10, 1976), 7.

8. *Oil and Gas Journal*, 68 (Jan. 26, 1970), 105.

PART 4

Improving Government Involvement in Consumerism Programs

CLIENT AND AGENCY REQUIREMENTS IN THE DESIGN OF CONSUMERISM PROGRAMS

Gerald Zaltman and Allan D. Shocker
University of Pittsburgh

Despite the apparent success of the consumerism movement, the authors wonder whether it has had an enduring effect on consumer behavior itself. They argue that it has not and then propose some criteria that might be established for designing successful programs directed at behavior change. In addition, structural changes in agency and client requirements are presented to facilitate the development of better programs.

For all the success the consumerism movement has had in achieving visibility, obtaining legislative and other action goals, and arousing the social consciousness of business, industrial, and government leaders, there is still legitimate question as to whether it has had an enduring effect on consumer behavior itself. The more conspicuous "successes" of consumerism have generally been those that limited choices consumers could exercise in the market, generally by imposing constraints on manufacturers and distributors. Certain products are kept off or removed from the market (product safety, pure food and drugs), certain features are mandated on some products (safety equipment and emission controls on automobiles, UHF receivers on television sets), or prohibited on others (unsafe product features, cyclamates in soft drinks), and so on. Importantly, much less success has accompanied efforts to affect consumers' abilities to protect themselves by their market behavior (consumer education, information disclosures, corrective advertising). While little evaluation research has taken place in these areas, the limited amount that has been conducted is generally disappointing in its support for the success of such programs. A few such program evaluations are described below.

125

Maisel et al. reported on a long-term program to evaluate various educational strategies designed to prevent accidental poisonings [9]. This long-term, multistrategy, geographically localized educational campaign had only a small effect on awareness and behavior change. Levy analyzed calls made to a St. Louis Drug Crisis Intervention Unit [7]. His article implies that a little information may be more dangerous than none, that various drug education programs seem to bring about only small increases in information and may produce unnecessary and unchanneled anxiety. Planek, Schupack, and Fowler evaluated the National Safety Council's defensive driving course in various states [12]. Using self-reported data, the study indicated that attendees had significantly fewer accidents than a control group. However, the reduction in officially recorded accidents was not sufficiently large to differentiate the study group from the comparison group that entered the course a year later. This suggests a response bias but no differences that could be attributed to the educational program.

Robertson and Haddon evaluated the impact of the buzzer light reminder system on automobiles [14]. No significant differences in seat belt use were found between those having the system (18 percent use) and those not (16 percent use). Note the low rate of use in either event. Robertson investigated the use of the safety belt interlock system mandated for 1974 model cars [13]. Use of seat belts under this condition was indeed higher (59 percent) than with the buzzer light system (28 percent). What is interesting is that only 59 percent of the people having the interlock system used seat belts, despite the effort, cost, and legal penalty risked to render the system inoperative. The interlock system was eventually abandoned, in part because of strong public sentiment against it. Robertson et al. compared use of seat belts between two groups using cable television, one receiving seat belt promotional messages and a control group not receiving the messages [15]. The program was judged a failure, recording "no measured effect whatsoever on safety belt use."

Day and Brandt examined the effect of information disclosure required by Truth-in-Lending legislation on knowledge of annual percentage rates and dollar finance changes and on credit purchase behavior over time [4]. They found that the improved knowledge of credit rates and charges that could reasonably be attributed to

Truth in Lending had relatively little effect on credit search and usage behavior. In spite of the dramatic improvement in consumer knowledge of interest rates, the majority of consumers remain uninformed and the least gains have been among the less affluent and poorly educated segments. Finally, Monroe and LaPlaca [10], Carman [3], and Ross [18], in reviewing a large number of studies conducted by independent researchers and by supermarkets on the use and costs of unit pricing, found that relatively large numbers of shoppers reported little or no use of unit pricing information. Those that reported using such information tended to be better educated, younger, employed, and to have large households.

The studies reported above and literally dozens of others indicate that attempts to increase knowledge, change attitudes, or alter behavior face formidable obstacles and are quite likely to result in failure or very little success. This research covers strategies ranging from being purely informational to those offering rewards or being punitive in character. Some were highly intensive, emotional and personal, while others were the opposite. It is to be stressed that successful consumer behavior efforts and others dealing with planned social change do occur. An analysis of such efforts reveals a fundamental knowledge of consumer behavior and the use of sound marketing principles, and suggests useful criteria regarding the conditions and actions that favor success.

The purpose of this paper is to sketch out briefly criteria for successful consumerism programs directed at behavior change, and to suggest the obstacles that often lead to such criteria not being satisfied during the design and implementation of such programs. The criteria to be presented are not exhaustive but appear to represent some of the more salient considerations for success.

CONDITIONS FOR SUCCESS OF PROGRAMS OF PLANNED BEHAVIORAL CHANGE

Recent efforts to broaden the concept of marketing [6, 8] suggest that a marketing problem exists whenever an organization or individual desires some particular behavior from a well-defined target population but possesses only limited ability to compel that behavior [20]. In such instances, the marketer must seek to affect the environment of that population in such a way that they will find it in their self-interest to pursue the desired behavior. It is relatively safe to assume that people follow their own self-interests, *as they define those interests.* The marketer must seek to determine what and how varied those interests are, how they can best be served (if at all) in a manner consistent with his own ends, and what factors in the customers' environments, personal and social, will enhance and detract from the success of his offerings.

The foregoing observations are directly applicable to the achievement of public policy and other social ends. Ultimately, they recognize consumer sovereignty and hence a limited ability to impose one's goals on others. The individual is generally the final arbiter of what he will or will not do with the resources at his command. When an advocate or agency or legislative body seeks to enforce its own view of the public interest or impose a majority will on a minority, it can do so to the extent it can affect the environment of the individual including the quantity of his resources. Consumers must accept safety belts on automobiles or do without automobiles. They can choose to dismantle or counter the intent of the belts but at additional cost or inconvenience. Many may thus choose to use the belts rather than bear these costs.

From such a vantage point, our approach will be to suggest a number of more specific criteria or conditions a consumerism or other change program should satisfy to be effective. Our first condition is:

1. *A program should be presented to consumers as being in direct response to a strongly felt need that can be satisfied without undue social, psychological, or financial cost.*

Evidence should exist for a perceived need for change in a substantial number of consumers before a program is undertaken. Consumer advocates and legislators supporting a program need to have objective research evidence and not simply their own judgment that a basic problem exists and a program is wanted by those intended to be served. There should be a willingness to follow the evidence and modify or even terminate a program if such need is found wanting.

Consumers exist in a social, psychological, economic milieu. They are immersed in social networks that serve as sources of example and encouragement or of apprehension and sanction. They possess different personalities and life styles, different intellectual and physical abilities, different ambitions and opportunities. They have unique limitations on their financial resources and existing commitments with which to contend. Not all consumers have the same needs or will approach a proposed change in the same way.

Research needs to be undertaken to define problems from consumer viewpoints, to separate symptoms from more basic causes and group them together in a logical way. Research can also help the planner assess the magnitude of the problem and explore existing courses of remedy. Perhaps a remedy available to all is only used by some. Greater awareness of such remedies may increase their use. Perhaps a remedy is little used because it is complex or expensive. Research can provide guidance to increase the efficiency or feasibility of such remedies. Greater understanding of customer viewpoints may help the planner anticipate dysfunctional consequences of proposed actions and understand the rationale of those consumer segments who would oppose some remedy.

Our second condition is:

2. *A change program should not be introduced unless consumers have or can very readily acquire the necessary capacity—cognitive, social, and economic—to accept it.*

The capacity of an individual or social system for change is a function of many interrelated factors. One's ability to learn new things depends on intellectual capacity, prior training, and experiences, as well as on self-confidence and other personal attributes. Different people may possess different psychological readiness for change or are prepared to assume different degrees of risk. Consumers have social relationships that embody previously existing norms. They occupy particular roles in connection with these relationships which influence the extent to which they can change or be changed by such norms. Expenditures of time and money may be more feasible for some than others, depending on the extent to which they control events or let events control them. Consequently, the existence of a need is not enough if the capacity for change is lacking. Consumers, for example, do not appear to have much information about nutrients; it is thus questionable whether many consumers could decode nutrient information or translate nutrient information into food mixes appropriate for the entire family.

The capacity to change should not be confused with motivation to change. People can be viewed as inherently pursuing their own self-interests as they define those interests. From such a view, one must seek to analyze motivation to change in terms of the relative benefits and costs perceived as relevant to the situation. The existing systems characterizing an individual's environment are generally purposeful; change, because it interferes with an existing design, may create some dysfunctional consequences for the individual or group. Emission control devices on automobiles, for example, may effect some perceptible change in the quality of the individual's environment and satisfy his collective social conscience, but they also may result in significant additional expense because of initial cost, maintenance, and the possibility of malfunction as well as reduced gas mileage and loss of power (reasons that may be more central to the individual's desire for car ownership). It is doubtful whether acceptance of such devices would have occurred voluntarily because of insufficient motivation to change. Further, the requirement of emission controls on new automobiles may have motivated some people to purchase used cars or repair existing ones. The issue of motivation brings us to our next condition, which is elaborated on below:

3. *The lower the degree of commitment to change among consumers, the more the need to make change easy for consumers to adopt or the greater the efforts made to heighten the commitment.*

Adoption of a proposed change is always aided by making the change simple, convenient, and as costless as feasible. When commitment is low, the need for facilitative strategies is great [25]. Existing research suggests some possibilities. Recent attention has been paid to applying information-processing research to public policy needs [22, 1]. For example, several research studies have demonstrated that individuals find it easier to make brand comparisons by attribute than by comparing all attributes for each brand. Russo et al. developed an in-store display that presents *for an entire product class* a listing of all brands and sizes together with their unit prices [19]. They have documented that such a system works effectively. This example could possibly be extended to other information contexts;

130

the researchers were able to use findings from behavioral studies to make information processing more convenient and so to enhance the probability that the information was actually used. Similarly, incentives—that is, a commodity or service provided for the performance of a particular act—have been used effectively in several health-related programs [11, 16]. Deniston attempted to raise middle- and lower-class high school students' general health knowledge [5]. The students were given both material and nonmaterial reinforcements to increase motivation to learn. From self-reported data, student health behavior improved. Knowledge levels also improved for both groups (lower- and middle-class students), and the gap between the two groups was lessened. The evidence indicated that the educational sessions alone were not sufficient to have achieved the desired results.

Incentives may not be necessary; self-interest may be enough to cause a change in behavior. But when motivation is otherwise lacking, promoting ease of use and providing incentives to increase self-interest can be effective. (Not incidentally, they may also be controversial.) The important thing once again is to recognize the distinction between consumer self-interest as the consumer defines that interest and consumer self-interest as defined by someone else in the role of consumer advocate or public policymaker. Where there is a discrepancy, the salient cost/benefit attributes of change as perceived by consumers should be determined and the plan for implementing the desired change amended to insure that dysfunctional attributes are minimized and positive ones capitalized on. This leads to our next condition concerning the design of a change program:

4. *Effective design of change programs should consider that consumers exist at any time in various stages of the adoption process.*

Social and individual change has been described by many people as an unfolding sequence of stages [17]. There is general agreement that different strategies may be relevant for particular stages [25]. Early stages usually require problem recognition efforts, while later stages require solution generation and implementation efforts. With regard to nutritional disclosure, for example, considerable information is to be presented about each product, principally because personal differences in nutritional needs preclude a single measure of its nutritional value. But a product high in vitamin content may also be high in calories or low in protein. Another product high in protein may also be high in calories or low in vitamins. When the levels of individual vitamins are separately identified, the decision problem may become quite complex for any but the most sophisticated consumers. For many people, the information would have its greatest value later, when enough individuals had passed through stages of problem recognition, diagnosis, and arousal or motivation to action and were seeking specific foods whose nutrients had been identified as particularly important for them. Thus, the degree of positive impact of nutritional disclosure on nutritional practices will vary directly as the proportion of consumers in later stages of knowledge increases. Unit pricing or gasoline mileage disclosures afford less complex information-processing tasks for many consumers, and thus the presence of the information may itself stimulate arousal.

There are other considerations in the design of social change programs, as indicated by the next two conditions:

> 5. *When designing a change program and its implementation plan, it is highly desirable to determine whether the intended adopters can be segmented into meaningful groups that might benefit from a differentiated program and/or implementation plan.*

Because different customers have different needs and capacities and different motivations to change behavior, it is frequently desirable to cluster consumers into meaningful groups and to differentiate marketing strategies for the different groups. Cultural attributes and economic, demographic, psychological, sociological, and geographic differences may help to define or at least recognize the differences between such segments. Thus, consumers may be grouped on the basis of ethnic, educational, social class, or regional considerations and addressed separately. Resistance to change may also be found in the form of cultural, social (including economic), and psychological barriers, so that realistic segmentation may cause the program developers to target their implementation efforts where benefits will be more realizable. For example, people may differ in the extent to which they feel able to influence or control those factors that affect them. Such beliefs may be deeply imbedded in culture. They may have profound effects on individual willingness to respond to a change program. In the U.S., such beliefs vary greatly according to income, age, sex, and many other factors that are more readily measurable. Selective perception and attention, significant reference group norms, status, and power position all may provide rational bases for developing some ability to predict resistance in specific cases and for developing appropriate segmentation strategies designed to reduce resistance or to target programs more efficiently.

6. *Effective programs of change require carefully orchestrated implementation plans in which care is given to the relative timing of each event both in terms of when an event occurs relative to other events and the amount of time an event requires to have an impact.*

An effective program of change requires care in execution. Prior to full-scale implementation of a program, a limited trial (test or pilot program) should be undertaken. An evaluation research component should be built into the design to permit constant evaluation of the program's impact and possible changes in the program's administration over time to improve its functioning. Such evaluation research should be begun sufficiently prior to implementation of the program to provide at least two benchmark studies. Every effort should be made to anticipate potentially undesirable consequences of a change program and to develop contingency plans for countering these consequences should they materialize. For example, consumers may feel that protection afforded by consumerist legislation is more comprehensive than it actually is and may, therefore, exercise less critical judgment. In the case of cooling-off periods on land purchases, this may result in greater rather than fewer numbers of initial commitments. A revision in the form or nature of the disclosure may be required.

The agency coordinating implementation may seek to design announcements of plans and disclosure of its evaluation results for major visibility through the news media. Background information may help stimulate awareness of the problem and the agency's proposed remedies or suggested consumer behavior. To the extent that consumer education must precede the desired behavioral change, the overall impact of the change program may be slow in coming. Efforts spent in simplifying the behavioral change required and in

133

preparing different materials for different segments of the population would pay dividends in reducing the time required for each phase of the change program. The evaluation research component would provide evidence of the rate of change as well as guidance to the proper timing of successive stages of the change program (e.g., an awareness campaign followed by information about use behavior and expected benefits).

CLIENT AND AGENCY REQUIREMENTS
FOR SUCCESSFUL CHANGE

For consumerist programs to be successful, they must meet legitimate customer needs and be compatible with their capacities and resources. Sometimes incentives may be necessary to enhance motivation. Behavioral support must be encouraged from existing social relationships and institutions. Planning and implementation of the programs must realistically assess the task to be accomplished and provide for sufficient information so that consumers at different stages in the adoption process can progress to later stages. In short, successful change programs present prescriptions for behavior to consumers in a manner that is as compatible as possible with their needs and desires, resources and capacities, and the social and cultural environment in which they find themselves. The agency must be prepared to undertake additional, differentiated strategies if a single one is not sufficiently compatible with these individual differences.

It would be easy to attribute the relatively low incidence of success for consumer change programs alluded to earlier to a lack of awareness of, or sensitivity to, the issues discussed above. At best this is only part of the story. We would be remiss if we were not sensitive to the situation faced by the consumer advocate or agency contemplating a change program.

As consumers were seen to be diverse, so also are consumer advocates. Generally such advocates represent particular causes; consequently each places high priorities on the achievement of his cause. Their identification and sources of support may come from others who ascribe to those causes. As a result, their interests may substantially differ from those of the public at large who do not have the same investment in the advocated position. Any contemplated change typically has multiple effects and ramifications because of the complex nature of society. (The authors recently were reminded of this when it was revealed that a movement by the airlines to increase the number of seats in coach sections at the expense of first class was being opposed by the National Basketball Association.) Consequently, some trade-offs must be made in the expected benefits and costs of change at the individual level. As each individual's situation is different, so also may be his reactions and behavior. There is no reason to expect that consumer advocates and other consumers will share the same goals, experience the same benefits or costs, or be otherwise compatible in their regard for a given position.

Much planned change takes place in government centers such as Washington and the state capitols. The tempo of life is noticeably rapid in such centers. Careers are made and broken within relatively short time spans. The people who are attracted to this environment are generally those who would thrive in it. The important concern is with gaining support for one's own programs and policies. People become advocates. Their orientation is toward action, not contemplation. Planning simply takes too long. The research necessary to design a beneficial program is often not available when the idea becomes important, and the impetus to push on will simply not permit the time to develop these inputs [23]. More importantly, the people who advocate a program generally are not those who must administer it or who must bear the costs of failure [21]. People may move on too rapidly to endure the full span of a program's implementation. Consequently, doing something plausible becomes more expedient than doing it well, and pragmatic issues become controlling.

Consumer advocates are normally well intentioned, but they must exercise their judgment as a pragmatic substitute for research. Wilkie and Gardner [23] have drawn on their observations as Federal Trade Commission staff to argue that the experience and training of those in positions of influence and policymaking lead to misconceptions about consumer behavior and, in turn, to poor judgment: Consumers should be interested only in the functional benefits of products rather than in their social or psychological benefits. The idea that a person would be willing to pay more for a certain brand even though

135

an almost identical functional product is available at a lower cost is thought to signal some flaw in the system or represent anticompetitive behavior on the part of business firms. Consumers are often thought to have considerable shopping time to make numerous comparisons, so that giving them more information will facilitate an economically rational decision. Little explicit recognition is given to the actual needs of consumers, the environment in which information is used, and the accumulation of relevant information through product usage, observation of the behavior of others, and word of mouth. Considerable consternation occurs when information provided consumers does not result in the intended behavior. (Serious consideration was once given to a ruling that would have greatly enlarged the size of health hazard warnings in cigarette advertising on billboards on the grounds that present warnings were not sufficiently conspicuous to passing motorists.) The power of advertising is generally overestimated. It is often perceived as capable in relatively short time periods of changing customer behavior. What is misunderstood is that for a commercial advertising campaign to be commercially successful, it is often necessary to change the behavior of only a very small percentage of all persons exposed to the advertising. The same percentage change resulting from a major consumerism program would not be considered successful.

The fact that many legislators and government policymakers were trained as lawyers leads them to view the world in advocacy terms. The attempt is to marshall all the evidence and reasoning in support of your position before the appropriate decision-making authority on the assumption that your opponent will do the same. Advocates are not necessarily concerned with being evenhanded or objective, and they rely on the opposition's behaving similarly to provide a balanced picture for consideration by the final decision authority. Consequently, the equality of organization and competence of both sides can strongly affect the decision rendered. When consumer interests are diverse and poorly stated or inadequately funded, the more organized special interests may be better able to achieve their ends.

A further consequence of this legalistic view may be the willingness to impose the advocates' standards of morality or public interest on consumers if there exists sufficient precedent in jurisprudence. Demonstration of actual customer use or benefit becomes almost incidental. Day and Brandt [4] and Ross [18] have noted the argument that an information disclosure requirement is justifiable simply if it enhances the customer's right to know. "Congress passed the [Truth in Lending] law on the issue of right to know rather than on any evidence of whether or not the consumer uses the information . . . . Congress was correct. The use the consumer makes of information is peripheral to the main issue of right to know." [2] Such a view also ignores consumer information-processing capabilities, as well as desired trade-offs between the amount of information presented and the prices of products (documentation and testing and the additional promotion required may raise the cost of goods). It often leads to poorly defined goals for change programs, thus creating ambiguity, uncertainty, and anxiety for those who are going to be affected by the change. Further, if goals are poorly defined, the change program cannot be evaluated in terms of its effectiveness in achieving those goals; therefore, appropriate remedial steps may be more difficult to take.

Finally, we would note that the structure of legal and social institutions exerts a major impact on the dimensions consumer programs can assume. Agencies such as the Federal Trade Commission or the Consumer Product Safety Commission have certain jurisdictions that may permit certain action alternatives and preclude others. Interagency cooperation is often less practical than is competition. If research were to indicate that a better way of enhancing the public's nutritional well-being would be to impose minimum nutritional standards for foods such as hot dogs, but the advocating agency was the Federal Trade Commission, the action chosen might be nutrient disclosure in advertising (disclosure on labels might fall partly within the jurisdiction of the Food and Drug Administration). Similarly, the legal system relies on the legislature for its ultimate authority. Yet the legislature may be unwilling for its own reasons to write laws in terms that will permit the courts greater jurisdiction and authority. This division of authority has ramifications not only for the remedies sought and the design of change programs, but also, for program implementation. Programs designed at the federal level may be implemented at the state or local levels by individuals who, having had no hand in the design, may have no commitment to making that design work. Being closer to consumers, they may even feel a program is ill-conceived or inadequate for the task and may actively thwart the implementation or develop implementation plans that conflict with policy guidelines

137

laid down in Washington. Delays, sanctions or threats of same, and, above all, confusion of consumers may result.

CONCLUSIONS

It is far easier to state problems than to provide solutions. The problems we have identified are age old and have often been discussed in separate contexts. The major remedies would, in the short run, appear to be piecemeal. Behavioral researchers working more closely with consumer advocates and policymakers may be better able to influence the design and implementation of action programs based on their understanding of consumer behavior. Conversely, researchers may better learn of activist thinking so as to channel their own research activities to provide the information needed to resolve basic questions that can be anticipated. Bettman [1] and Wilkie [22], among others, have sought to condense a broad body of behavioral research to fit more adequately the needs of public policymakers. Other researchers have taken the initiative of consulting policymakers for their ideas and requirements before finalizing their own research designs [24]. The FTC some years ago hired a number of behavioral scientists interested in consumer problems to serve in an in-house advisory capacity [23]. Such programs might be expanded and extended to other agencies, and permanent staffing might be contemplated. Analyses of program costs and benefits and a program of evaluation research might be required of any policy recommendation sent by staff for approval.

In the longer run, structural changes will probably be desirable to broaden the jurisdiction of public agencies or to promote interagency cooperation. Greater funding for basic behavioral research relevant to consumer problems might be provided through mechanisms such as the National Science Foundation or a separate consumer research agency or funding authority. Greater efforts might be made to encourage private sources of research funding through universities or quasi-independent organizations such as the Marketing Science Institute. If public agencies were to provide early indication of issues under consideration, enlightened private self-interest might lead to more research support with requirements of public disclosure.

Technological developments may make direct customer inputs to planning of public policy initiatives more feasible. Electronic voting devices attached to television sets may make such consumer research less expensive and the information more timely. Research on human information processing and multiattribute decision making may provide researchers with improved ability to predict consumer reactions to public policy initiatives [20] and a useful conceptual framework for cumulating a more enduring understanding of the whys and wherefores of that elusive being, the consumer.

REFERENCES

1. Bettman, James R. "Issues in Designing Consumer Information Environments," *Journal of Consumer Research,* 2 (Dec. 1975), 169-77.

2. Bymers, Gwen. "Seller-Buyer Communication: Point of View of a Family Economist," *Journal of Home Economics,* 64 (Feb. 1972), 59-63.

3. Carman, James M. "A Summary of Empirical Research on Unit Pricing in Supermarkets," *Journal of Retailing,* 48 (Winter 1972-73), 63-71.

4. Day, G. S. and W. K. Brandt. "Consumer Research and the Evaluation of Information Disclosure Requirements: The Case of Truth-in-Lending," *Journal of Consumer Research,* 1 (June 1974), 21-32.

5. Deniston, O. L., I. M. Rosenstock, and V. A. Getting. "Evaluation of Program Effectiveness," in H. C. Schulberg, A. Sheldon, and F. Baker, eds., *Program Evaluation in the Health Fields.* New York: Behavioral Publications, 1969.

6. Kotler, Philip. "A Generic Concept of Marketing," *Journal of Marketing,* 36 (Apr. 1972), 46-54.

7. Levy, R. M. and A. R. Brown. "Untoward Effects of Drug Education," *American Journal of Public Health,* 63 (Dec. 1973), 1071-3.

8. Levy, Sidney J. and Gerald Zaltman. *Marketing, Society, and Conflict.* Englewood Cliffs, N.J.: Prentice-Hall, 1975.

9. Maisel, G., et al. "Analysis of Two Surveys Evaluating a Project to Reduce Accidental Poisoning Among Children," *Public Health Report,* 82 (June 1967), 555-60.

10. Monroe, Kent B. and Peter J. LaPlaca. "What are the Benefits of Unit Pricing?," *Journal of Marketing,* 36 (July 1972), 16-22.

11. Mushkin, Selma J., ed. *Consumer Incentives for Health Care.* New York: Prodist, 1974.

12. Planek, T. W., S. A. Schupack, and R. C. Fowler. "An Evaluation of the National Safety Council's Defensive Driving Course in Various States," *Accident Analysis & Prevention*, 6, 271-97.

13. Robertson, L. S. "Factors Associated with Safety Belt Use in 1974 Starter-Interlock Equipped Cars," *Journal of Health and Social Behavior,* 16 (June 1975), 173-7.

14. _____ and R. Haddon, Jr. "The Buzzer-Light Reminder System and Safety Belt Use," *American Journal of Public Health,* 64 (Aug. 1974), 814-5.

15. _____, et al. "A Controlled Study of the Effect of Television Messages on Safety Belt Use," *American Journal of Public Health,* 64 (Nov. 1974), 1071-80.

16. Rogers, Everett M. *Communication Strategies for Family Planning.* New York: The Free Press, 1973.

17. _____ and Floyd Shoemaker. *The Communication of Innovations.* New York: The Free Press, 1971.

18. Ross, Evan. "Applications of Consumer Information to Public Policy Decisions," in Jagdish N. Sheth and Peter L. Wright, eds., *Marketing Analysis for Societal Problems.* Urbana: Univ. of Illinois, 1974, 42-76.

19. Russo, J. Edward, Gene Krieser, and Sally Miyashita. "An Effective Display of Unit Price Information," *Journal of Marketing,* 39 (Apr. 1975), 11-19.

20. Shocker, Allan D. and V. Srinivasan. "Proactive Approaches to Implementing the Marketing Concept: A Review of Multi-Attribute Applications to Product Concept Generation and Evaluation," working paper #145, Graduate School of Business, Univ. of Pittsburgh, 1976.

21. Stefflre, Volney J. *New Products and New Enterprises: A Report of an Experiment in Applied Social Science.* Irvine: Univ. of California, 1971.

22. Wilkie, William L. *Assessment of Consumer Information Processing Research in Relation to Public Policy Needs.* Washington, D.C.: U.S. Government Printing Office, 1975.

23. _____ and David M. Gardner. "The Role of Marketing Research in Public Policy Decision Making," *Journal of Marketing,* 38 (Jan. 1974), 38-47.

24. Zaltman, Gerald, et al. "Product Satisfaction and Safety: A Comparative Analysis of the Elderly and Other Segments of the Population," Unsolicited research proposal submitted to the National Science Foundation, Graduate School of Business, Univ. of Pittsburgh, 1976.

25. _____ and Robert Duncan. *Strategies for Planned Change.* New York: Wiley Interscience, 1977.

CONSUMER PRIORITIES AND EVALUATION OF GOVERNMENT INVOLVEMENT IN VARIOUS CONSUMER PROGRAMS

E. Laird Landon, Jr.
University of Houston

Ralph L. Day
Indiana University

The authors believe that little attention has been devoted to measuring the priorities consumers assign to the activities carried out by government for their benefit. This paper reports on an effort to measure and evaluate consumer priority rankings and assessments of seven major forms of government activity. A better understanding of consumer priorities should lead to improved government responsiveness.

As interest in consumerism has grown in recent years, some interesting research has been done on consumer attitudes toward marketing practices and the role of government in marketing [1]. However, relatively little attention has been devoted to measuring the priorities consumers assign to various alternative kinds of activities carried out by government for their benefit. Also neglected is the extent to which consumers feel that these activities are being given the appropriate amount of emphasis by government at the present time. This paper reports a recent effort to measure and evaluate consumer priority rankings and assessments of current efforts for seven major forms of government pro-consumer activity. The data are from a section of a lengthy questionnaire that was a preliminary version of the data collection instrument to be used in a large national survey of consumer satisfactions and dissatisfactions being conducted by the Office of Consumer Affairs, Department of Health, Education and Welfare [3, 4, 5].

The questionnaire was distributed to an area probability sample of residents of Boulder, Colorado. From the 400 households specified by the design, 275 usable responses were obtained. The non-responses resulted from the failure to locate about 40 of the selected units, refusals by about 55 units, and failure of about 30 respondents to correctly complete their questionnaires. Although the limited nature of the sample suggests caution in making any generalizations from the results, the findings are interesting and appear to be potentially useful.

ACTIVITIES, PRIORITIES, AND THE GOVERNMENT'S ROLE

An assessment of both the priorities assigned to consumer activities carried out by government agencies and the extent to which the respondents believe that government is presently emphasizing these activities was made. The seven activities were identified as follows:

1. Consumer education in elementary and high schools
2. Product information labeling (as on food, drug, and household products)
3. Product testing and reporting to the public
4. Preventing misleading advertising
5. Protecting the consumer's health and safety (auto safety, health warnings on cigarette packages, etc.)
6. Helping consumers who have complaints about products or services
7. Establishing minimum quality standards for products

Subjects were asked to "indicate the degree of emphasis you would place on each of these" by ranking them from 1, indicating the greatest degree of emphasis, to 7. After they had rank ordered the statements, respondents were asked to indicate "how strong a part you think the government should play in each of these areas" by marking one of the following responses: "Government is doing *too little* now; . . . the right amount now; . . . *too much* now."

The Priority Rankings

The results show a considerable difference of opinion across the sample with respect to which of the seven activities should be given the highest priority. The activity given the highest priority by the largest number of respondents, "product testing and reporting to the public," received 22.8 percent of the first-place votes. The activity given the highest priority by the smallest number of respondents, "helping consumers who have complaints about products and services," received 8.4 percent of the first-place votes. The other five activities received percentages of first-place votes ranging from 11.6 to 17.1, as compared with an expected percentage of 14.3 under the asssumption of equal emphasis across the population. While the observed pattern of assignments of rankings, as shown in Table 1, does not reveal an extremely high level of agreement on priorities, priority assignments were far from equal. Each column individually, each row individually, and the complete 7 X 7 contingency table were tested against the uniform distribution by X^2 and all were statistically different at the .05 level of significance.

The seven activities are presented in Table 1 in the order (declining) of first-priority rankings. While the number of first-place rankings is a useful starting point in assessing the results, it does not tell the full story. The number of lowest priority ratings an activity receives is also revealing. One would expect an activity that is high in first-place rankings to be low in last-place rankings and vice versa. This was true for "product testing," which had 78 first-place choices and only 4 last-place choices with the number of choices gradually declining over the range, indicating considerable agreement among the respondents. Quite the contrary occurred with respect to "consumer education in elementary and high schools." Although it received the second largest number of first-place votes (59), it had by far the largest number of last-place choices (79), with the remaining choices rather evenly spread over the intervening five levels. The priority rating patterns of the other five items reflect varying degrees of agreement.

Because the data are in the form of rankings, it is not strictly appropriate to compute means and other statistics that assume that the data have interval scale properties. The median is appropriate for ordinally scaled data but is not especially helpful in situations such as the present one in which large numbers of identical responses are assigned to a small number of ranks. The median ranks for the seven items are shown in the right-hand column of Table 1. The seven items can be grouped by median ranks and placed in rank order to

TABLE 1

PRIORITY RANKINGS OF ACTIVITIES FOR THE BENEFIT OF CONSUMERS

Activities	Rankings							No Answer	Mean Rank	Median Rank
	1	2	3	4	5	6	7			
Product testing and reporting to public	78	55	43	42	27	13	4	13	(1) 2.77	2
Consumer education in public schools	59	25	22	26	25	29	79	10	(5) 4.27	4
Minimum quality standards	55	51	43	36	17	37	24	12	(2) 3.44	3
Preventing misleading advertising	43	40	53	37	46	30	13	13	(3) 3.55	3
Information labeling	41	46	32	41	56	34	14	11	(4) 3.69	4
Health and safety warnings	40	26	31	24	34	44	64	12	(7) 4.42	5
Helping consumers with complaints	29	25	34	39	45	47	45	11	(6) 4.39	5

N = 275.

provide some measure of summarization. With the understanding that the results should be interpreted with care, the means of the rankings were computed as well. These are also shown in Table 1, along with the rank order of the mean ranks (in parentheses).

By whatever means of evaluation one might wish to apply, it is clear that "product testing and reporting to the public" is the activity to which the largest number of respondents gave the greatest emphasis, since it had the most "1s," the fewest "7s," and the lowest median and mean. It is equally clear that the two activities "health and safety warnings" and "helping consumers with complaints" received the least emphasis. "Minimum quality standards," "preventing misleading advertising," and "product information labeling" were fairly closely grouped together in the middle. The most controversial item was "consumer education in schools," which was number two in terms of highest emphasis rankings, dead last in terms of the number of lowest emphasis ratings, and fifth in terms of mean rankings. This suggests that there is a moderate-sized segment of the population that feels consumer education is extremely important, while the rest of the population fails to regard it as a high-priority activity. Unlike the other six cases, more than half of those giving priority ratings to this item were concentrated at the two extremes rather than being distributed over the entire range in a more or less regular pattern.

Some interesting conclusions are suggested by the results as presented in Table 1 and briefly discussed above. The first is that the priorities assigned by the respondents do not seem to reflect the degree of emphasis currently being placed either by consumer advocates or by government consumer protection agencies. The issues stressed by consumerists have been the handling of consumer complaints and the protection of the consumer's health and safety. These activities were given the least emphasis by our sample. Much emphasis has been placed by consumer protection agencies, especially the Federal Trade Commission (FTC), on the prevention of false and misleading advertising and on requiring companies to provide more information on product labels. These two activities were ranked in the middle by the respondents. The two top items on the basis of mean ranks, "product testing and reporting" and "establishing minimum quality standards," have not been stressed by the consumerism movement as much as the other items. The consumer priorities data also suggest that there is far less agreement on what activities should be stressed than many consumerists might think. Perhaps the data will suggest to consumerists that they should begin to do "market segmentation research" to identify homogeneous groups and learn why their priorities differ. The following discussion of the respondents' evaluations of government's efforts with respect to the seven activities and the later analysis of respondents' attitudes should shed some additional light on this issue.

146

Evaluation of Government Activities

The rank orderings of the various activities discussed above were designed to reflect the respondent's personal judgment about the degree of emphasis that *should be given* to each activity. After they had ranked the seven activities on this basis, the respondents were asked to make a judgment about the degree to which the government is *actually performing* these activities at the present time. The responses of "too little," "the right amount," and "too much" are implicitly related to the respondent's own notion of the appropriate levels. In other words, the respondent was not assessing his priorities in this subsection but was evaluating the extent to which present government activities are consistent with his priorities. In a sense, the respondent was assessing his satisfaction with the government's performance, and it is quite possible that one could feel the government was doing too little on an activity that was given a low priority and doing too much on an activity that was given a high priority. The objective was to obtain an assessment of the performance of government with respect to the seven activities, with the priorities reflected in the previous subsection as the frame of reference.

The results reveal a rather strong feeling among the respondents that, in general, government is doing far less than it should with respect to the seven activities for the benefit of consumers. The results are presented in Table 2, with the activities listed according to the number of "too little" responses each received. Excluding the "don't know, no opinion" responses, 65 percent of those expressing opinions selected "too little," 30 percent selected "the right amount," and 5 percent indicated that "too much" was being done. For five of the seven activities, more than 70 percent of those responding indicated that too little was being done. The two exceptions were "product information labeling" and "health and safety warnings." Only for the latter activity did as many as 50 percent of the respondents indicate that the government was doing the appropriate amount. It was also the only activity for which more than 5 percent of the respondents indicated that the government was doing too much.

The pattern of "don't know, no opinion" responses evident in Table 2 reflects a considerable variation over the seven activities. The most notable is "consumer education," for which 109 of the

147

TABLE 2
EVALUATION OF GOVERNMENT'S PERFORMANCE

Government is doing . . .

Activities	Too Little	The Right Amount	Too Much	Don't Know	No Answer
Preventing misleading advertising	197 (78.1%)	52 (21.1%)	2 (0.8%)	16	8
Product testing and reporting	188 (76.8%)	52 (21.6%)	5 (1.7%)	25	5
Establishing minimum quality standards	165 (71.6%)	54 (24.0%)	10 (4.4%)	40	6
Helping consumers with complaints	165 (79.0%)	35 (17.1%)	8 (3.9%)	62	5
Consumer education in public schools	130 (81.0%)	22 (13.9%)	8 (5.1%)	109	6
Product information labeling	124 (49.2%)	122 (48.4%)	6 (2.4%)	16	7
Health and safety warnings	74 (28.1%)	138 (53.5%)	48 (18.4%)	10	5
TOTAL	1043 (64.7%)	475 (29.9%)	87 (5.4%)	278	42
Mean	149.0	67.9	12.4	36.9	6.0

269 respondents (40 percent) gave a "don't know" response. This might mean that the concept is poorly understood relative to the others and/or that respondents lack sufficient knowledge about what the government is actually doing to make a judgment. The large number of first-place priority rankings for "consumer education"

148

suggests that it is understood and valued by a substantial segment of the population. The even larger number of last-place rankings and the rather even distribution over the intermediate ranks might mean that another segment of the population is relatively unfamiliar with the concept and ranks it last by default. In five of the seven activities, the pattern of responses for those who did express an opinion was very similar, with roughly three-fourths of the responses in each case loaded on the "too little" answer. The two exceptions were "product information labeling," with responses approximately equally loaded on "too little" and "the right amount"; and "health and safety warnings," with 28 percent on "too little," 54 percent on "the right amount," and 18 percent on "too much." The proportion of "don't know" responses was quite low for both of these items.

Possible Implications

The rankings data indicate a rather clear rank ordering of priorities over the seven activities. A clearly bimodal pattern occurred only in the case of "consumer education in schools." It is notable, however, that no single activity received a dominant share of the first-priority rankings, and none failed to received a substantial share of first-priority rankings. It is also notable that two protectionist activities, "helping consumers with complaints" and "health and safety warnings," were at the bottom of the rankings, and information-type activities such as "product testing and reporting" and "consumer education in schools" were at the top. These data suggest that consumers would prefer more emphasis on activities that would help them make better decisions in the marketplace rather than protect them from shady practices or from themselves.

When subjects evaluated the extent to which the government is actually performing the seven activities, they were answering a different question and used a different scaling method. Thus, it is not inconsistent with the rankings to see that "preventing misleading advertising," which was fourth in terms of first rankings and third in terms of the mean rank, received the most "too little" answers. This simply reflects that more people felt the government was doing less than it should for this activity than for any other activity. "Helping consumers with complaints," which was at the bottom of the priority rankings, was tied for third place in the number of "too little" ratings.

149

These results suggest that the two subsections of the questionnaire were indeed, as intended, measuring two different dimensions: (1) consumers' priorities with respect to government activities for the benefit of consumers, and (2) consumers' evaluations of whether or not these activities are being carried out at the appropriate level. The results suggest that there was far from uniform agreement over the sampled population as to which of the seven activities should be stressed. The performance evaluation results suggest that there was rather general agreement that government should perform the various activities at higher levels than at present, with the exception of "health and safety warnings," for which the majority indicated that the appropriate amount of this activity was now being done.

MULTIVARIATE ANALYSIS USING ATTITUDINAL DATA

In addition to the priority rankings and assessments of the emphasis being placed by government on the seven consumer programs, the questionnaire included a section designed to measure respondents' attitudes toward various matters of concern to consumers. The rest of this paper will be devoted to our efforts to use some of the methods of multivariate statistical analysis to identify relationships between the respondents' attitudes, as measured by our battery of 48 numerically scaled items, and their priority rankings and assessments of current government activities.

Attitude Scales

The attitude items were related to business in general, specific marketing practices including advertising, government in general, government and business relationships, specific government practices, sources of consumer information, and the various decision strategies available to consumers. The scales were "Likert-type," requiring the respondent to agree or disagree with a verbal statement using a five-point numerical scale. The numerical responses were keyed to levels of agreement, with 1 meaning "strongly disagree" and 5 meaning "strongly agree." The exact wording of each statement is given in the Appendix, so that the items can be referred to by number only or by number and abbreviated statement in the following text and tables.

150

Responses were distributed over the five levels for all items, and patterns of response varied widely over the items. The mean level of response varied from a low of 1.92 to a high of 4.18. The median of the item mean was 2.95, very close to the midpoint of the scale. The items with the highest means (reflecting agreement with the statement) were 9, 45, 47, 7, and 27. These included two statements critical of advertising, one calling for the establishment of minimum quality levels by government, one supporting the use of both list prices and actual prices by discounters, and an acknowledgment that consumers must share the responsibility for their buying mistakes. The lowest mean levels occurred for items 12, 4, 48, 10, and 13, reflecting disagreement with statements suggesting that the lowest priced items are always the best buy, that the highest priced item is always the best buy, that consumers aren't interested in unit prices, that consumers don't read informational labels, and that advertising leads to lower prices. In general, the results suggest that respondents tended to be highly critical of advertising, to favor some kinds of government intervention, to desire more product and price information, and to have a fairly sophisticated view of price/quality relationships.

Factor Analysis

In an effort to find an underlying "simple structure" in the 48 individual items and to identify a smaller set of composite variables for further anaysis, the attitude data were factor analyzed. Principal components were extracted with the BMD X 72 program, using squared multiple correlations as the commonality estimates. Twenty-nine factors had positive eigenvalues and these accounted for 49 percent of the total variance. The ten factors with the highest eigenvalues were rotated, using the Varimax criterion. These ten factors accounted for 39 percent of the total variance.

Factor scores were generated for the ten factors. When these were used in multiple regression analysis to predict priority rankings, none of the regressions were significant and the largest multiple R-square was .07. Because of the apparent complexity of the relationships among the attitude items and the small amount of total variation

151

accounted for by the major principal components, no further effort was made to use factor analysis.

Multiple Regression on Rank Orders

Because many of the attitude items appear to have more or less obvious relationships with one or more of the seven consumer programs, it seemed appropriate to regress the individual items on the rankings for each of the seven programs. Summary information on each of the seven regression analyses is given in Table 3. Only the items with relatively high beta weights are shown in order to conserve space. The multiple correlation, squared multiple correlation, and significance level are also given for each regression. The regressions explain between 23 percent and 29 percent of the variance in the respective program rankings, and all regressions are significant beyond the .01 level.

Space does not permit item-by-item discussion of the regression results. However, careful examination of the results in Table 3 for each of the seven programs can provide useful insights. The frequency of appearance of items related to the role of government, business-government relationships, and the individual's role in politics is especially notable. An effort to draw some overall implications will be made in the Conclusions section below.

Multiple Regression on Government Effort Ratings

Regression analyses were also performed with respondents' ratings of the present level of government effort as the dependent variable. Respondents evaluated each of the seven consumer programs by indicating whether too little, the right amount, or too much is currently being done. While this form of response may make the assumption of an interval scale a heroic one, the advantage of using regression and the exploratory nature of the study led us to make this assumption. The results of the regression analyses can be compared to the foregoing analysis of the priority rankings more easily than if a technique based on a nominal-scaled dependent variable were used. Table 4 presents a summary of the results. As in Table 3, only the items with high beta weights are shown. It can be seen that the regressions on government effort ratings explain considerably more of the variance in these assessments than did the regressions on priority rankings. The percentage of explained variance ranges from 49 to 58.

Again, space does not permit item-by-item discussion of the regression results, but careful examination of the results in Table 4 can provide useful insights. It is notable that many more of the attitude items achieved sizable beta weights and that marketing-related issues were considerably more prominent than was the case with the regressions or priorities rankings. In other words, government-business relationships and the individual's role in political activities do not appear to be as highly related to assessments of present government efforts as they were to the assignment of priorities. An effort to draw some overall conclusions will be made in the following section.

CONCLUSIONS

Because this study was exploratory, no firm conclusions are warranted. However, the data do suggest some interesting relationships. If these relationships can be confirmed in further research, a better understanding of consumer priorities may lead to improved government responsiveness. The following paragraphs suggest some hypotheses that seem to follow from the results reported in this paper.

Priorities for Government Consumer Activities Are Differentiated

Considerable support appears to exist for all programs studied in this research. Helping consumers with complaints, which received the fewest first-place ranks, still received 8 percent of all first-place ranks as compared to an "expected level" of 14.3 percent. Even in a relatively homogeneous community such as Boulder, Colorado, real differences of opinion exist as to where the government should place its highest consumer priority. The federal government's relative lack of success in launching an integrated consumer program may result from the difficulty in agreeing on just what needs to be done. Each government program may be responding to a separate public. What is more confusing, each program may be dividing effort among many publics.

TABLE 3

ATTITUDE ITEMS WITH LARGEST BETAS FROM REGRESSIONS WITH RANKING OF EACH CONSUMER PROGRAM

Consumer Program/Items	Beta	Multiple R	MR^2	F	Number of Items in Regression
Consumer Education in Schools		.477	.227	.006	32
7. Government should set minimum quality standards	.25				
19. People are responsible for bad government	.22				
15. We can wipe out political corruption	.19				
Product Information Labeling		.543	.294	.000	28
22. Advertising results in better products	−.28				
10. I never read package labels on food value	.21				
23. The average citizen can influence government decisions	−.23				
Product Testing and Reporting		.541	.293	.000	34
14. Advertised products are more dependable	−.26				
39. Advertisements are reliable sources of information on quality	.24				
36. Advertisements present a true picture of products	−.21				
20. I usually don't read ingredients list on packages	−.21				

154

	Beta				
Preventing Misleading Advertising		.526	.276	.276	34
10. I never read package labels on food value	-.25				
18. I often pay the higher prices in convenient stores	-.17				
15. We can wipe out political corruption	-.16				
Protecting Consumer's Health and Safety		.486	.236	.007	34
12. Best buy is the cheapest	-.22				
31. The world is run by a few people in power	.22				
42. Business has too much influence on government decisions	.17				
Helping Consumers with Complaints		.493	.243	.002	32
32. We are the victims of uncontrollable forces	-.20				
29. Government controls advertising well	.18				
21. Business provides good products at reasonable prices	-.17				
23. The average citizen can influence government decisions	-.16				
Establishing Minimum Quality Standards		.538	.289	.000	26
7. Government should set minimum quality standards	-.49				
34. Government has too much control over business	-.21				
42. Business has too much influence on government decisions	-.19				
31. The world is run by a few people in power	.18				

N = 234 for each regression. Item wording is abbreviated. Complete items are in the Appendix. Attitude items are scaled from disagree (1) to agree (5), and ranks are scaled from high priority (1) to low priority (7). Therefore, a positive beta weight suggests that agreement with the item leads to a low priority.

155

TABLE 4

ATTITUDE ITEMS WITH LARGEST BETAS FROM REGRESSIONS WITH EFFORT RATINGS OF EACH CONSUMER PROGRAM

Government Program/Items	Beta	Multiple R	MR^2	F	Number of Items in Regression
Consumer Education in Schools		.764	.584	.001	37
20. I usually don't read ingredients list on packages	.41				
7. Government should set minimum quality standards	-.28				
39. Advertisements are reliable sources of information on quality	-.28				
21. Business provides good products at reasonable prices	-.28				
36. Advertisements present a true picture of products	-.26				
Product Information Labeling		.728	.530	.004	35
8. Businessmen are as honest as other people	.34				
36. Advertisements present true picture of products	-.29				
47. A discount store price tag should show manufacturer's list price	-.28				
24. I often buy in neighborhood stores although I pay more	-.26				
13. Advertising results in lower prices	-.25				
Product Testing and Reporting		.733	.522	.025	39
25. The environment is more important than our living standards	-.38				
20. I usually don't read ingredients list on packages	-.34				
1. You learn about new products by buying and trying them	.28				
21. Business provides good products at reasonable prices	.26				
29. Government controls advertising well	.26				
Preventing Misleading Advertising		.701	.492	.035	37
19. People are responsible for bad government	.38				
29. Government controls advertising well	.38				
38. I get shopping tips from friends	-.24				

Protecting Consumer's Health and Safety

.721 .520 .004 34

Item	
43. Consumer advocates have not done much for the consumer	.31
23. The average citizen can influence government decisions	.25
22. Advertising results in better products	-.24
18. I often pay the higher prices in convenient stores	-.22

Helping Consumers with Complaints

.759 .575 .003 39

Item	
1. You learn about new products by buying and trying them	.40
42. Business has too much influence on government decisions	.35
21. Business provides good products at reasonable prices	.33
43. Consumer advocates have not done much for the consumer	.31
22. Advertising results in better products	-.31
37. People can control world events by taking an active role	-.30
32. We are the victims of uncontrollable forces	-.29

Establishing Minimum Quality Standards

.738 .545 .005 37

Item	
47. The price tag in a discount store should show manufacturer's list price	-.36
35. People have little control over what politicians do in office	.33
22. Advertising results in better products	.33
17. I'll pay a little more for brands I can trust	.30
21. Business provides good products at reasonable prices	-.28

N = 102 for each regression. A large number of respondents indicated no opinion. Effort ratings are scaled from "too little effort" (1) to "too much effort" (3). Therefore, a positive beta weight suggests that agreement with the item leads to a rating toward the too-much-effort end of the continuum. Since a relatively small percentage of the sample indicated too much effort (see Table 1), the effective range of the scale is "too little" effort to "about right" effort.

Present Government Effort Is "Too Little"
for Consumer Activities

These data seem to indicate that the government should do more than it presently is, regardless of overall program priority. With the exception of product information labeling and health and safety warnings, all programs received about the same number of "too little" responses. It is not clear, however, how much money consumers want spent on these programs. Mary Wells Lawrence has suggested that if a consumer were given $100 and asked if s/he would prefer to keep it or give it to the government for consumer protection, most, if not all, would choose to keep the money. The point is that the format of the level of effort question does not adequately present costs and other trade-offs. The continuing struggle by consumerists to establish a federal consumer agency seems, at least in part, to be a battle over what cost is appropriate.

Attitudes Concerning Government Consumer
Programs Are Diverse

The factor analysis of 48 consumer attitude items indicates that they cannot be readily reduced to a few key predictors. The ten best composite factors accounted for only 39 percent of the variance in the 48 items. Said another way, most of the items measure separate attitudes and understanding their role in program priorites may be difficult.

Consumer Attitudes Are Related to Priority
and Effort-Level Ratings

The regression analyses reported here show only moderate levels of prediction of the dependent variable. For priority rankings, only 23 percent to 29 percent of the variance in the seven programs was explained by the attitude items. For effort-level ratings, 49 percent to 58 percent of the variance was explained by the attitude items. However, the regressions do not appear suitable for use in a predictive sense because of the large number of items in the equations (28 or more for each equation). It does not appear that any one univariate attitude construct is likely to explain enough of the variance to merit an intensive research effort, if the objective is prediction. In seeking to understand the priority and effort-level responses, the regression results are helpful. However, with so many items contributing, the data are difficult to analyze. It seems more appropriate to hypothesize relationships between specific attitude constructs and a specific dependent consumer program, and then to design a study to test the hypothesis. While prediction may not be immediately improved, understanding should be increased.

Political Fate Control Attitudes Are Related
to Consumer Program Rankings

The several items from the Collins scale of Political Internal-External Locus of Control [2] seemed to be relatively important in several regressions. It appears that ratings of program priorities and present activity levels may be considerably influenced by general attitudes toward government. Other studies have concentrated on attitudes toward business [1], but not attitudes toward politics.

While these attitudes may relate to rankings of programs, it is not clear what the underlying dynamics are. With some programs, "internal" items are related to high-priority ranks; with others, they are related to low-priority ranks.

Government Effort Levels and Attitudes
Toward Business

Some of the data support the notion that favorable attitudes toward business and advertising are positively related to support for more government effort with consumer programs. While the data are somewhat equivocal, this notion is contrary to traditional wisdom. It may not be only the cranks and the disenchanted who support federal programs. On the contrary, it may be that many more of those who believe in the present political and business systems are motivated to favor increased government activity.

All of these hypotheses need to be developed further and rigorously tested in future work. These generalizations, if supported, may improve understanding of consumer priorities for government involvement in the marketplace. Such understanding can contribute greatly to increased government efficiency.

APPENDIX

Items Used to Measure Consumer Attitudes Statement

1. The best way to learn if new products are good is to buy them yourself and try them.

2. The government should control food prices.

3. Advertising helps raise our standard of living.

4. The most expensive model is usually the best value.

5. I value my personal time more than the savings I could make by shopping around.

6. I usually like to see how other people like new brands before I try them.

7. The government should set minimum standards of quality for all consumer products.

8. Businessmen in general are as honest as other people.

9. Advertising often persuades people to buy things they shouldn't buy.

10. I never read the information about vitamins and other nutritional values on food packages.

11. I never check the grade on the label when I buy meat or canned vegetables.

12. You usually get the best buy by buying the cheapest.

13. In general, advertising results in lower prices.

14. In general, advertised products are more dependable than unadvertised ones.

15. With enough effort we can wipe out political corruption.

16. Competition assures that consumers pay fair prices.

17. I would rather pay a few cents more and get brands I can trust.

18. Many times I pay higher prices in convenient stores because it isn't worth it to me to make a special trip.

19. In the long run the people are responsible for bad government on a national as well as a local level.

20. I usually don't read the list of ingredients on packages of the products I buy.

21. Business performs the job of providing good products at reasonable prices very well.

22. Advertising results in better products for the public.

23. The average citizen can have an influence in government decisions.

24. I frequently buy in my neighborhood stores even when I know I am paying more than I would at discount stores.

25. Protecting the environment is more important than maintaining our standard of living.

26. You can usually trust what a salesperson in a retail store tells you about the merchandise you are shopping for.

27. Many of the mistakes consumers make in buying products result from their own carelessness or ignorance.

28. I don't pay a lot of attention to advertising.

29. The government does a good job of controlling advertising.

30. It is better to buy from a reputable dealer than one who offers the lowest prices.

31. This world is run by a few people in power, and there is not much the little guy can do about it.

32. As far as world affairs are concerned, most of us are the victims of forces we can neither understand nor control.

33. One of the major reasons why we have wars is because people don't take enough interest in politics.

34. The government has too much control over business.

35. It is difficult for people to have much control over the things politicians do in office.

36. In general, advertisements present a true picture of products advertised.

37. By taking an active part in political and social affairs, the people can control world events.

38. I like to get shopping tips and advice from my friends.

39. In general, manufacturers' advertisements are reliable sources of information about the quality of products.

40. I just don't have the time to hunt for information on the different brands when I buy a new appliance.

41. People should be allowed to decide for themselves if they want seat belts and shoulder harnesses when they buy a new car.

42. Business has too much influence on government decisions.

43. Consumer advocates such as Ralph Nader get a lot of publicity but have not done much for the consumer.

44. There should be a law preventing door-to-door selling.

45. Most advertising insults the intelligence of the average consumer.

46. I depend a lot on information I get from articles in magazines when deciding what to buy.

47. When shopping in a discount store, I like to see the manufacturer's list price on the price tag in addition to the actual price.

48. The total price of an item is what I'm interested in, not the price per ounce.

REFERENCES

1. Barksdale, Hiram C. and William R. Darden. "Consumer Attitudes Toward Marketing and Consumerism," *Journal of Marketing,* 36 (Oct. 1972), 28-35.

2. Collins, Barry E. "Four Components of the Rotter Internal-External Scale: Belief in a Difficult World, a Just World, a Predictable World, and a Politically Responsive World," *Journal of Personality and Social Psychology,* 29 (Mar. 1974), 381-91.

3. Day, Ralph L. and E. Laird Landon, Jr. "Collecting Comprehensive Complaint Data by Survey Research," in Beverlee B. Anderson, ed., *Advances in Consumer Research,* Vol. 3. Cincinnati: Assn. for Consumer Research, 1975, 263-8.

4. _____ and _____. "Survey Data on Consumer Complaints for Consumer Protection Policy Makers," *Proceedings Midwest American Institute for Decision Sciences,* Indianapolis, Ind., 1975, 40-4.

5. Landon, E. Laird, Jr. and Ralph L. Day. "The Need for Better Data on Consumer Complaints," *Colorado Business Review,* 48 (Mar. 1975), 2-4.

PART 5

Future Perspectives on Consumerism

A TEN-YEAR AGENDA FOR CONSUMER ADVOCATES

Lee Richardson
Louisiana State University

This paper is concerned with the direction of the consumer movement in the next decade. Relying on a review of the history of consumerism, the author sets forth a ten-point agenda for supporters of consumerism. The agenda itself is entirely normative.

The consumer movement in the United States has shown considerable activity since the mid-1960s. Similar social movements in behalf of consumers have not been durable, however, and the lessons of history do not provide clear indications of the direction and intensity of consumerism in the next decade.

Lest normative prescriptions for the movement be entirely wishful thinking, it is necessary to revisit previous U.S. experience. The patterns of the periods 1900–1914 and 1930–1939 reveal many similarities to the 1962–1976 phase. The third period, however, promises to go beyond the cyclical developments of the earlier two. These developments should logically form the basis for the objectives of the movement in the next decade.

While resources for further meaningful advances of consumerism as a social, political, and economic force in American society may be directed toward the goals outlined, there are uncontrollable variables that may upset the program. These underpinnings of the agenda for consumer advocacy are the historical forces that changed and stunted previous waves of consumerism in the United States.

HISTORY OF U.S. CONSUMERISM

Hermann [7] has identified three periods of consumerism in the U.S.:

A. 1890–1914
B. 1930–1939
C. 1960–Present

Significant similarities can be found between each of these periods. The following elements are common to all and have been identified in part by Hermann and others [1, 5, 7].

Similarity of Issues

Food has traditionally been the largest single element in consumer expenditures. The Pure Food and Drug Act was signed on June 30, 1906, became a major issue of reformers in the 1930s, and is a dominant issue of consumer groups today. Food prices launched nationwide supermarket picketing in 1966 [13]. The U.S. Department of Agriculture (USDA) and the Food and Drug Administration (FDA) have consistently been at the center of the debate over food sanitation, prices, and U.S. agricultural policy [4, 7].

Drugs, medicines, and related health issues also have historically been themes of consumerism. The Pure Food and Drug Act of 1906 was enforced first against a patent medicine called curforhedake brane-fude, a concoction that did not feed brains or cure headaches [4]. In 1937, 93 pint bottles of ELIXIR sulfanilamide killed 107 people and led to the strengthening of the 1906 act one year later [7]. Thalidomide caused several thousand birth defects and led to a 1962 amendment to the 1906 act, giving the FDA more authority over new drug introductions.

Advertising regulation was given a major boost by the passage of the 1914 Federal Trade Commission (FTC) Act. The model Printers Ink Statute (1911) and early self-regulation of advertising by the pre–World War I precursors of today's Better Business Bureaus are instances of concern with this prominent aspect of marketing. The Wheeler-Lea Act (1938) strengthened FTC efforts against deceptive advertising. Truth in Lending (1968) and numerous FTC cases against advertisers [11] have affected that industry in the third phase of consumerism.

Federal Government Involvement

The FTC, FDA, and USDA are three agencies consistently at the forefront of consumer controversy. As the federal government has expanded enormously, the involvement of more federal departments has followed. One federal self-study in 1961 showed 33 agencies affecting consumer interests [17]. A 1976 booklet lists over 50 sources of consumer services [15].

Curiously, there has been no development of a central consumer agency in the federal government, although a department of consumer affairs has been proposed [14]. Similarly, the Congress passed bills creating an independent consumer agency in 1975, but the President threatened to veto such a proposal. The concept of representation in individual federal agencies has been implemented in various short-lived forms since the 1930s [1, 4, 14].

CONSUMER ADVOCATES

Numerous individuals and private organizations have been involved in lobbying and in the public advancement of consumer interests as they perceived them. Among the individuals of note are public officials as well as private citizens:

DR. HARVEY W. WILEY—A Purdue chemistry professor, who resigned because the university trustees disapproved of his bicycle riding, and become the USDA's crusading advocate of the Pure Food and Drug Act.

UPTON SINCLAIR—The author of *The Jungle,* a novel featuring filth in the Chicago meat packing industry, whose readers so pressed the Congress and President Roosevelt that the Pure Food and Drug Act was law five months after the book was published [4].

F. J. SCHLINK—A writer whose coauthorship of books (*especially Your Money's Worth,* 1927, and *100,000,000 Guinea Pigs,* 1932) and whose founding of Consumers Research (1929) made him a key figure in the consumer movement of the 1930s.

169

COLSTON E. WARNE—An economist who founded Consumers Union in 1935 as a result of a split within Consumers Research; his product-testing organization has been the largest U.S. private consumer interest group since 1936.

REXFORD G. TUGWELL—A USDA official who patterned himself after Harvey W. Wiley in the 1930s phase of consumer activism.

RALPH NADER—The dominant private citizen reformer of the 1960s and 1970s and founder of several organizations.

ESTHER PETERSON—A grocery store executive who has contributed to the movement primarily since 1960 as a presidential consumer affairs advisor, as president of the National Consumers League, and as an innovator of consumer-oriented business practices.

Many of the leading advocates overlap phases of the consumer movement. Wiley was active in public life for a half century until 1930. Schlink headed Consumers Research in the 1970s, although his influence has waned. Warne has been a leading spokesman of consumers for four decades. Peterson's public activities in the 1940s and 1950s were also important.

Consumer organizations, often affiliations of leading individual advocates, sometimes overlap the phases of historical activity:

National Consumers League (D.C.) 1899–Present
Consumers Research (N.J.) 1929–Present
Consumers Union (N.Y.) 1935–Present
New Jersey Consumers League (N.J.) 1900–Present
Consumer Federation of America (D.C.) 1967–Present
Conference of Consumer Organizations (Ariz.) 1974–Present
National Consumers Congress (D.C.) 1973–Present

All of the above are national in scope except the New Jersey Consumers League. Consumer Federation of America has 208 organization memberships (which in turn have over 30 million members) only, whereas the others all have individual members ranging from a few hundred (Conference of Consumer Organizations) to over two

170

million (Consumers Union—technically, each subscriber to its magazine is a member, although only a minority use their voting membership rights).[1]

The multiplicity of consumer organizations at the national and state levels, especially in the 1930s and the current phase, belies their weakness in budgets and staffing. Consumers Union's resources, the largest in staff (over 300) and budget (over $20 million), are primarily devoted to its magazine. The Consumer Federation of America has less than 10 staff members and is the largest of the national organizations devoted to advocacy instead of product-testing magazines (Consumers Research and Consumers Union). Several advocacy groups affiliated with Ralph Nader have no memberships but do have larger staffs and budgets than the Consumer Federation of America.[2]

---

[1]The consumer interest groups are not all clearly identifiable as such. The Cooperative League of the U.S.A. and many labor unions have secondary priorities advocating consumerist positions. The Community Nutrition Institute is a consumer-oriented food issue group. The American Council on Consumer Interests is an academic association devoted to research in consumer problems. The Center for Science in the Public Interest is a consumer group specializing in science-related subjects. Most state and local consumer groups are affiliated with the Consumer Federation of America and thus reveal their generally similar interests at least on national issues. The Movement for Economic Justice and Environmental Action are but two of many public interest groups with certain subject area specializations (energy and electric utilities in these instances) that result in joint efforts with the consumer movement groups.

[2]Ralph Nader has been given credit for starting 20 advocate groups [6]. The central organization is the Center for the Study of Responsive Law. The key lobbying agency is Congress Watch. Fundraising activity is led by Public Citizen. Students are organized in several states through Public Interest Research Groups. Groups such as Critical Mass (nuclear power moratorium) and the Agriculture Accountability Group represent specialized subject efforts.

PUBLICITY AND THE MEDIA

The small size of consumer advocacy organizations is compensated in part by the enormous media interest in consumer advocates' points of view.

Publicity for *The Jungle,* as well as the book itself, contributed to the longer-term efforts of Harvey Wiley's publicized "Poison Squads" in passing the Pure Food and Drug Act [4]. The elixir sulfanilamide and thalidomide scandals were prominent in the media. The supermarket boycotts of 1966 were major features in the newspapers [13]. Ralph Nader's actions are followed closely by the press and constitute an important part of his success formula [6]. Interest in consumer journalism reached a high point with the publication of *Media and the Consumer* in the early 1970s (publication ceased in 1975), a monthly publication that analyzed the treatment of consumer problems by the media, particularly newspapers.

History's Questions

The similarities of the three consumerism phases demonstrate little more than those similarities. The ten-year forecast of the direction and intensity of consumer movement activities cannot assume identical events. The first two phases were interrupted by World Wars I and II; the nation evidently turned its energies away from consumer issues to higher priorities.

It does not follow that a cyclical history of consumerism portends a decline in the movement again. Neither does it follow that only military priorities can cause the demise of interest in these issues; war may not come, and other external events could interrupt. Other forces also may be operating to influence the direction of modern-day consumer movement activities.

FRAMEWORK FOR THE AGENDA

Given some heroic assumptions, such as no major historical turning points that will interrupt the forces apparently producing the consumer movement, the outlines of a feasible program for consumer advocacy for the next decade become visible. There are several key historical underpinnings that lay the bases for the ten-year agenda of consumer leaders. They should be made explicit:

1. Continuation, if not increase, in the role of government in marketing activities and the economy. While constantly criticized, government continues to gain major regulatory assignments that affect consumers.

2. Continuation of the desire of the consuming public to eliminate fraud, deceit, and one-sided market transactions favoring sellers. Presumably, consumerism is based on undesirable marketplace events.

3. Continuation of the reality that there remains a lot of fertile, unworked political ground for exploitation by consumer advocates. Many important industries have not yet been subject to major scrutiny by the movement.

4. Expectation that no radical change will occur to revolutionize private enterprise's basic control of investment and operating decisions in the vast majority of U.S. industries. Consumerism would undoubtedly be altered in a socialist economy, for example.

5. Expectation that the U.S. standard of living and distribution of income will not radically change. Some maintain that the movement is a product of an affluent society.

6. Expectation that no other factor will upset the current cycle of interest in consumer affairs, especially in view of its recent historical peaks of institutionalization in business, government, and the professions. This is the "all others" assumption necessary when forecasting social change. For example, consumer leaders could become scandalized or advocate unpopular causes. Similarly, a counterforce could develop and stifle the movement.

THE AGENDA

The agenda is entirely normative even though set in the context of historical experiences and lessons. The limited resources of the consumer movement further restrain growth and order particular priorities for the future.

Each item of the ten-point agenda is set forth with an explanation of its importance. Each priority has its positive aspect for supporters of the objectives of consumerism—and, concomitantly, its negative aspect for those seeking the demise of the movement. More positivist scholars should question the validity of any item, but they might find the listing useful as a basis for evaluating the progress of consumerism during the next several years.

The agenda reads as follows:

1. *Creation of a central federal consumer office for advocacy, research, and policy analysis.*

The Agency for Consumer Protection (Consumer Protection Agency and Agency for Consumer Advocacy in other congressional bills in the past) will advance the consumer interest in several ways:

a. Increased legal leverage to gain access to the policymaking process in thousands of federal agencies, divisions, and subunits
b. Centralized responsibility in the federal system, to enable public interest groups and the consumer constituency to focus attention on one primary unit
c. Relative independence from the Executive Branch through budget, Senate approval of the administrator, and statutory responsibilities

2. *Creation of a central private national organization that gains wide public recognition much as Ralph Nader has achieved as an individual.*

The private consumer movement does not have a primary national organization with high public visibility. While poorly staffed and funded, the many small organizations only further weaken the movement. The largest public interest concern is personified in Ralph Nader more than any central consumer advocacy group. Labor, business, farm, and other producer interests have more than a single representative organization each, so that each of these economic forces has been able to muster resources to develop strong multiple advocate groups.

Centralization of the consumer movement necessarily forces compromises by leaders of the separate movement groups. While they already cooperate in many areas such as certain subject specializations and joint lobbying efforts,[3] unity is undoubtedly strength. Necessary to the successful joining of several existing organizations is the assumption that federal, state, and local projects all can be undertaken by a single group. Currently, consumer groups in the aggregate pay a great deal of attention to state and local matters that differ in substance from national issues.

3. *Establishment of forceful and widespread consumer education programs in the nation's educational system.*

Consumer education is a powerful idea; yet it is an evolving phenomenon rather than a movement as described by Bloom and Silver [2]. There is no national consumer education advocacy or professional organization. There is a small federal office of consumer education buried under layers of Office of Education superstructure and higher priorities.

Nonetheless, consumer education takes place in schools, community programs, and the media nationwide [3, 9, 12]. Essentially, the consumer movement can expect a higher degree of support from an informed consuming public. Consumer education activities should increase awareness of consumer problems and willingness to institute the social, political, and economic changes necessary to correct those problems.

---

[3]Examples of specialization are the energy and food activities of the Center for Science in the Public Interest, product evaluations by Consumers Union, and automobile safety investigations by Ralph Nader. The Agency for Consumer Protection, consumer credit legislation, and condemnation of U.S. agricultural polices are constant concerns of many groups.

175

A major response of many consumers to the appeals of the consumer movement has been total apathy. The sparse funding and limited memberships of the consumer groups testify to the classic and chronic problem of a diffuse political interest [8]. Of course, "informed consumers" might not have parallel interests with existing consumer organizations, and indeed they could cause consumerism to take major new directions. On the other hand, consumer education, like much other education, reflects many of the values of the existing society; therefore, it is less likely to reject the concepts of advocates should they become numbered among society's most prominent leaders. They certainly are not so numbered today.

4. *Completion of the process of state and local government takeover of the third-party role as mediator and resolver of consumer complaints, as source of state and local consumer news, and as consumer advocate in state and local affairs.*

Unknown generally is the widespread development of state and local public consumer offices. Estimates of their number are difficult because some are part-time appointive functions of a single individual associated with a mayor or other local official. All states have some state-level office, and many have specialized state-level units such as consumer counsels for representation of residential utility customers or consumer complaint officers in insurance and other departments. In any event, state and local units combined probably number over 300 [16].

The major functions of these offices are handling complaints, supplying consumer information (education), and providing policy advice, although some have statutory rule-making, licensing, or other powers. Their further development appears assured and the potential numbers of state agencies and local jurisdictions (there are more than 3,000 counties in the U.S.) suggest that a major new form of public administrator—the consumer professional—may evolve first at the state and local level rather than in the federal system.

5. *Establishment of new and revised mechanisms of efficient public input into the increasingly complex government-business interfaces of the next decade.*

Although there are several generally accepted approaches to the increasingly significant joint ventures and regulatory relationships between the private and public sectors, there are no standard, comprehensive methods that appear to achieve the levels of participation desired by public interest groups. The methods in use today, and those recommended for the future, are:

a. *Sunshine methods.* The Consumer Product Safety Commission, for example, not only keeps records of its officials' contacts with businesses, but it even posts them in advance. The Freedom of Information Act amendments of 1974 provide for a relatively simple process of disclosure of government documents upon citizen request. Congressional lobbyists must register.

b. *Consumer representation.* The Agency for Consumer Protection, consumer advisory committees, and agency consumer offices are several of the standard means of representation. Lesser known is the Federal Trade Commission's limited direct funding of public interest groups whose views the FTC wishes to have presented. Another variation is the Consumer Product Safety Commission's funding of certain groups who appear capable of proposing product safety standards.

c. *Limiting business relationships.* Prohibitions can be developed to prevent certain types of contacts. Federal officials can be stopped from meeting with industry representatives except under certain conditions such as in the presence of Department of Justice legal counsel. Officials can be prohibited from accepting expense reimbursements from business (a common practice in the federal government). Business representatives can be refused appointments to certain advisory councils and commissions subject to conflicts of interest. Corporate contributions to politicians is an area where restrictions already exist. Federal officials can be prevented from obtaining future employment in certain industries. Business executives can be prohibited from entering government at the policymaking level in regulatory agencies related to their industries.

6. *Breakthrough for at least one major new representation mechanism that will provide consumers with direct policymaking power in corporations.*

There has been little development of this option. Consumers and businesses are seen as adversaries in many instances, and adversaries traditionally do not welcome each other into positions of power in their own camps. The consumer movement has little reason to believe it can achieve a major breakthrough by voluntary actions of businesses.

There are, however, several possibilities for consumer representation in business, although there is little momentum for any of them at this time.

    a. *Federal corporate charters.* As legal creations, corporations could probably be better controlled by federal charter processes than by the less powerful state governments. Consumer influence would be felt through the federal government.

    b. *Government ownership of business.* This is not a serious proposal for general reform at this time. There is consumer group support for federal health insurance and federal involvement in petroleum ventures. The Tennessee Valley Authority, the Alaskan Railroad, and the Postal Service are other examples of special purpose government economic enterprise in the U.S.

    c. *Corporate board changes.* German corporations have mandatory labor representation. Supervisory boards could be created to review operating boards' activities. Much as women and minorities have pressured and gained management sponsorship for broad memberships, other interests could do likewise.

    d. *Corporate consumer offices.* Such units exist in vast numbers, usually with limited public relations, consumer information, and complaint-handling functions. Few companies seek consumer input through high-level management appointments, paid consumer advocate consultations,[4] consumer advisory committees, and other means more commonly found in government but also appropriate for industry groups and individual enterprises.

---

[4]Consumer advocates functioning as consultants to industry create conflicts of interest, yet this is happening with increasing frequency.

7. *Development of working public service concepts in the professions and their further separation from employers in government and business.*

Professions traditionally view themselves as capable of independent action, yet, they are often criticized as captives of their clients. Professional opinions of lawyers or accountants, for example, have certain legal standing. Lawyers and doctors have legally sanctioned privacy in their client relationships, and journalists vehemently seek similar rights in law.

A limited tradition of public service at little or no cost to clients can be attributed to many professions. However, *pro bono* public service outside of professional circles is not common among business people, scientists and others whose donated services could be immensely useful to the consumer interest—not the least of which might be the reordering of some priorities and substantive policy positions.

Achievement of this agenda item is complicated by the insular nature of most professions. To the extent that a profession perceives itself to be independent, it is less likely to be receptive to pressure from external sources, including public interest groups or even government. This is particularly true for accounting [10], and medicine opposes government-proposed peer review standards for individual decisions of doctors. The professions are understandably inclined to believe they are the best prepared technically to set their own standards of performance.

8. *Civil service protection for public-spirited bureaucrats— including "whistle blowers."*

Whistle blowers are those persons who publicly announce their disenchantment with their employers [9]. Government whistle blowers are subject to a variety of sanctions from their agencies, which no doubt limits the practice of public-spirited disloyalty. There is evidence, however, that other potential employers will not necessarily ally with the original employer, so that resignation in protest is less likely to mean premature retirement than a temporary career interruption [18].

9. *Development of a group of interdisciplinary substantive consumer affairs professionals in business, government, and other institutions to improve the quality of "consumerist" programs and policies.*

Many of the other items on the agenda will help foster consumer professionalism. More agencies and larger consumer organizations mean more job opportunities. On the other hand, there have been few actual professional developments such as the following:

a. *Professional societies.* The fledgling society of Consumer Affairs Professionals in Business is beginning in industry. The American Council on Consumer Interests is a society of academic research professionals. Consumer advocates do not have any large scale council or society. Public agency employees are attempting to develop a national association, but it is not assured of a successful launch.

b. *Professional training.* University degree programs specifically in the consumer affairs field are beginning slowly (Cornell, Alabama, Wisconsin, Illinois, California at Davis, among others). In-service training is largely a matter of chance except for the University of Wisconsin's (Milwaukee) Center for Consumer Affairs' frequent sponsorship of workshops and conferences since 1963. Thus, training is mostly on the job, through trial and error, or by successful application of other training and education to consumer affairs.

10. *Development of a full range of substantive topical and industry specialists in organizations and as individuals to work in behalf of consumers in relatively unexplored areas. These might include energy policy, insurance, financial institutions, antitrust policy, and the delivery of education.*

This agenda item follows directly from the fact that consumer groups have too few resources to meet their objectives, and from the assumption that consumerists, like mining companies, will frequently discover problems where they choose to explore and dig for them. The specific problems and needs for reform are matters for speculation at this time.

IMPLICATIONS OF THE AGENDA

The lessons of history are often perceived selectively to render them harmless. The forecasting of directions for a complex social movement built on such perceptions multiplies the hazard. Finally, to prescribe methods of steering social forces through unknown future conditions threatens a writer's credibility.

Compensating the tribulations inherent in such a trial attempt to help direct consumerism is the postulate that the effort is worth the undertaking. The consumer movement may eventually benefit in some small degree.

REFERENCES

1. Aaker, David A. and George S. Day, eds. *Consumerism,* 2nd ed. New York: The Free Press, 1974, Introduction.

2. Bloom, Paul N. and Mark J. Silver. "Consumer Education: Marketers Take Heed," *Harvard Business Review,* 54 (Jan.-Feb. 1976), 32.

3. *Consumer Education Materials Project.* Mt. Vernon, N.Y.: Consumers Union, 1972.

4. Faber, Doris. *Enough.* New York: Farrar, Straws & Giroux, 1972.

5. Gilmartin, Jeanine. "An Historical Analysis of the Consumer Market," Doctoral dissertation, Georgetown University, 1970.

6. Gorey, Hays. *Nader.* New York: Grossett & Dunlap, 1975.

7. Hermann, Robert O. *The Consumer Movement in Historical Perspective.* University Park, Pa.: Dept. of Agricultural Economics and Rural Sociology, Pennsylvania State Univ., 1970.

8. Nadel, Mark V. *The Politics of Consumer Protection.* New York: Bobbs-Merrill Co., 1971.

9. Nader, Ralph, Peter Petkas, and Kate Blackwell, eds. *Whistle Blowing.* New York: Bantam Books, 1972.

10. Nelson, Carl L. "Review of Abraham Briloff, More Debits than Credits," *Business Week* (Mar. 8, 1976), 12.

11. Preston, Ivan L. *The Great American Blow-up.* Madison, Wis.: Univ. of Wisconsin Press, 1975.

12. Richardson, Lee. *Consumer Education: State of the Art.* Washington, D.C.: U.S. Office of Education, 1976.

13. _____. "Mass Communications and the Consumer Movement," in Lee Richardson, ed., *Dimensions of Communication.* New York: Appleton-Century-Crofts, 1969.

14. Troelstrup, Arch W. *The Consumer in American Society,* 4th ed. New York: McGraw-Hill Book Co., 1970, Chaps. 16-18.

15. U.S. Department of Health, Education and Welfare, Office of Consumer Affairs. *Guide to Consumer Services.* Washington, D.C.: U.S. Government Printing Office, 1976.

16. _____. *State Consumer Action-74.* Washington, D.C.: U.S. Government Printing Office, 1975, vii.

17. U.S., House of Representatives, Committee on Government Operations. *Consumer Protection Activities of Federal Departments and Agencies.* Washington, D.C.: U.S. Government Printing Office, 1961.

18. Weisband, Edward and Thomas M. Franck. *Resignation in Protest.* New York: Grossman Publishers, 1975.

CONSUMERISM IN THE YEAR 2000: THE EMERGENCE OF ANTI-INDUSTRIALISM

Paul N. Bloom
University of Maryland

Louis W. Stern
Northwestern University

The authors argue that consumerism as it exists today will dis-appear from the American scene. They believe it will be replaced as a major social movement by a convergence of forces that they call "anti-industrialism." The paper explores these forces at length, and indicates the kinds of issues that will be paramount in this new move-ment.

By the year 2000, it can be predicted, the consumerism movement as it has evolved in the decades of the 1960s and 1970s will be dead. In its place, a new movement—centered on anti-industrialism—will emerge and capture the consciousness of concerned individuals. The latter movement will encompass issues far more compelling in scope and impact than those addressed by the former; therefore, it is likely to have a more lasting effect on the way in which societal problems are solved and decisions are reached. The seeds of this change in focus are already present. They can be found in the present-day orientation of some consumerists and in the underlying discomfort of those not directly concerned or preoccupied with consumerism issues. In fact, the trends in the consumerism movement indicate that a process of creative destruction is taking place that will, by the year 2000, lead individuals to attain a higher level of awareness of and control over the forces structuring the world in which they live.

THE DECLINE OF THE CONSUMERISM MOVEMENT

The survival of a social movement is dependent, to a great extent, on the movement's ability to generate "ideas in good currency" [15]. The consumerism movement has been able to grow and prosper over the last two decades because it has been remarkably successful at suggesting policies and programs that appeal to a large cross-section of the American people.

Among the most widely accepted ideas generated by the consumerism movement is the notion that a variety of public and private organizations are needed to protect and assist consumers. Consequently, a large number of government agencies and private organizations have been established in recent years to work for the interests of consumers, and many more organizations of this type can be expected to develop in the near future. In the short run, these organizations and their employees should provide the consumerism movement with a strong political power base that will help it push through a considerable amount of new legislation. This *institutionalized consumerism* should, however, eventually contribute to the decline of the consumerism movement, because organizations, especially those initiated by federal, state, and local governments, historically have not been very adept at generating "ideas in good currency." Organizations are, by nature, conservative and tend to become preoccupied with self-preservation [15]. Government organizations, in particular, often become client-serving bureaucracies that cater to the needs of a very small constituency [17]. Furthermore, organizations are prone to acquiring the characteristics of those institutions with which they are in conflict [16].

One can, therefore, envision the development of a bureaucratic network of consumer organizations that would cater to the needs and wants of their employees and a small group of "clients" (e.g., consumer educators, consumer affairs personnel). Such organizations would increasingly ignore, as many business firms have done, the more basic and pressing needs of the majority of American consumers. In other words, when institutionalized consumerism becomes widespread, a consumerist bureaucracy will develop that will focus its concern on problems that will seem trivial to most Americans— particularly if the trends discussed in the next section continue to develop.[1] For example, it will be extremely difficult for consumer organizations to generate much interest in such matters as the absence of price tags on grocery items (due to the adoption of automated supermarket checkout systems) when most people have become increasingly anxious about such problems as radioactive contamination of their drinking water or worldwide food shortages. In fact, consumer problems will likely be viewed by most people as issues that can be dealt with on an individual basis, rather than as matters that demand collective protest on a mass scale.

It is not intended to imply here, however, that, by the year 2000, consumers will no longer be concerned about such matters as deception in advertising, shoddy workmanship, high-pressure sales tactics, and poor service. Consumers will be just as angry in the future (if not more angry) when they feel they have been taken advantage of. However, consumers will be more prone to take actions *on their own* to obtain restitution or redress from sellers who have treated them poorly. They will complain more visibly, more vocally, and more frequently, and they will file more lawsuits. An "age of litigation" (see [14]) may even develop if underemployed lawyers begin to seek out more business from angry consumers. This *individualized consumerism* will be spurred on by several trends, including the rise of individualism in American society [2], the diffusion of consumer education programs that will teach consumers where and how to complain and sue [3], and the growth of the service sector of the economy [1]. The last trend will increase the number of seller-consumer confrontations, because sellers of services will have more personal contact with their customers than sellers of tangible goods; and such closeness and familiarity will breed contempt.[2]

In gist, institutionalized consumerism combined with a desire to handle the traditional consumerism problems on an individualized

---

[1]It is also possible that public concern with consumer problems will diminish because of progressively more creative response by business firms to consumerism. Business firms could give consumerists what they want (i.e., safety, information, a voice, and a choice) without giving in on more global concerns.

[2]The current medical malpractice suit crisis may be a harbinger of things to come in the service industries.

basis will probably lead to the end of the consumerism movement as we know it today. These new forms of consumerism will not produce nearly as much public controversy or social change as consumerism forces have produced in the past. The consumerism movement will likely experience a fate similar to that of the labor and civil rights movements. While there still will be many organizations and activists presumably working for the interests of the buying public, both the amount of support received by them as well as their rate of progress will be substantially reduced.

THE RISE OF ANTI-INDUSTRIALISM

It can be predicted that, by the year 2000, widely-supported and highly active anti-industrialism movement will emerge to fill the void left by the consumerism movement. In fact, such a movement should be highly appealing to many of today's consumerists; a number of them have essentially been anti-industrialists all along, while others are likely to become increasingly disenchanted with the consumerist bureaucracy's tendency to focus on trivial issues.[3] In addition, the occurrence of certain industrialism-induced crises, such as cata-strophic accidents in nuclear power plants, could also impel some consumerism organizations to change their focus entirely. However, it is expected that the anti-industrialism movement will attract much of its support from people who were never actively involved with the consumerism movement. (Conversely, many former consumer activists may find it difficult to support anti-industrialism because of its innate antagonism toward the way in which economic resources are presently organized and allocated.)

The Nature of Anti-Industrialism

The United States has clearly become the world's most *industrial-ized* society. It is a society that relies heavily on the efficient opera-tion of large-scale, technologically advanced, industrial enterprises

---

[3] It could be argued that Ralph Nader himself has already become an anti-industrialist. He has been concerned recently about nuclear power plants and federal chartering of corporations and has given only lukewarm support to the bill that would establish an Agency for Consumer Advocacy.

to satisfy the needs of its citizens. Moreover, it is a society that looks toward rapid technological and industrial growth as a means of satisfying more needs in the future. The government of this society actively encourages and supports improved industrial efficiency and continued technological and industrial growth through a wide variety of policies and programs. And the individual citizens of this society, after years of being urged to increase their productivity and their consumption of goods and services, generally contribute to industrial efficiency and growth by adhering to the Protestant Ethic and by maintaining their consumption patterns.

Dissatisfaction with American industrialism has, of course, surfaced on untold numbers of occasions. The recent consumerism movement is one of a long series of movements (e.g., populism, socialism, environmentalism) that have pointed out flaws and problems with American industrialism [13]. But unlike many of the other movements, the consumerism movement has rarely questioned the fundamental premise on which American industrialism is based: the desirability of technical efficiency and of technological and economic growth. Instead, the consumerism movement has focused most of its attention on such problems as the lack of product safety or of adequate consumer information made available by the industrial system. The anti-industrialism movement that will likely emerge to replace the consumerism movement will, in contrast, devote its energies to seriously questioning the desirability of continuing to stress efficiency and growth.

The comparisons provided in Table 1 should help clarify how anti-industrialism will differ from consumerism. As the table indicates, thus far the consumerism movement has focused most of its efforts on helping consumers achieve the four basic consumer rights identified by President Kennedy: the rights to safety, to be informed, to be heard, and to choose. Considerable pressure has been exerted on the American industrial system to produce safer products, to provide more consumer information, to pay more attention to consumer complaints and desires, and to allow consumers to choose from a reasonably large assortment of products and services.

On the other hand, the anti-industrialism movement will seek:

- The *survival* of society, rather than merely the safety of consumers

TABLE 1

COMPARISON OF THE OBJECTIVES OF THE CONSUMERISM MOVEMENT AND THE ANTI-INDUSTRIALISM MOVEMENT

The Consumerism Movement Seeks:	The Anti-Industrialism Movement Will Seek:
Safety	Survival
Information	Knowledge
A voice	Power
A choice	Authority

- *Knowledge* about the complexities of society, rather than merely information about the attributes of goods and services
- *Power* to influence the decisions that will affect the future of society, rather than merely a voice in making these decisions
- The *authority* to make decisions concerning what goods and services will be made available to whom, rather than merely the opportunity to choose from an adequate number of offerings

This new movement will seek knowledge, power, and authority to allow it to control industrialism in a manner that would theoretically insure the survival of American society and improve the overall quality of life for all citizens. Indeed, anti-industrialism will provide at least one superordinate goal—survival—around which diverse and previously conflicting segments of society can coalesce.

In reality, this movement may already be well on its way to becoming a major force in American society. According to W. W. Harman, Director of Stanford Research Institute's Center for the Study of Social Policy:

> The basic paradigm that has dominated the industrial era (including emphasis on individualism and free enterprise; ma-

188

terial progress; social responsibility mainly the concern of the government; few restraints on capital accumulation; etc.) . . .

and that involves striving toward such goals as efficiency, productivity, continued growth of production and consumption, continued growth of technological and manipulative power . . .

has resulted in processes and states (e.g., extreme division of labor and specialization, cybernation, stimulated consumption, planned obsolescence and waste, exploitation of common resources) . . .

which end up counteracting human ends (e.g., enriching work roles, resource conservation, environmental enhancement, equitable sharing of the earth's resources). The result is a *growing and massive challenge to the legitimacy of the present industrial system.* [9]

The Substance of Anti-Industrialism

Table 2 contains a listing of some of the major trends that should lead the anti-industrialism movement to become an influential and widely supported force in American society. All of these trends have been discussed extensively elsewhere, so only a brief discussion of their nature and implications is presented below.

Perhaps the most obvious trend that should bring about the rise of anti-industrialism is the growing scarcity of indispensable resources such as energy, food, and certain minerals. Population growth, and the economic growth that must accompany it, should gradually deplete "spaceship earth's" [4] supply of precious resources to dangerously low levels. At the same time, environmental pollution, caused by efforts to improve industrial efficiency and growth, should turn clean air and water into increasingly scarce commodities and, possibly, aggravate the scarcity situation with respect to food. The dimensions of these growing scarcity problems have, of course, been documented in frightening detail by numerous writers [6, 7, 18].

To overcome the growing problems of scarcity and pollution, it will be necessary in the future to place even greater reliance on technological developments. Technology will be called on to find more efficient ways of using scarce resources, additional sources of

189

TABLE 2

SELECTED TRENDS THAT SHOULD LEAD TO THE RISE OF ANTI-INDUSTRIALISM

Environmental Trends

- Growing scarcity of:
  - energy
  - food
  - key minerals
- Increasing levels of pollution

Technological Trends

- Increasing reliance on technology to:
  - improve efficiency
  - provide energy, food, and key minerals
  - eliminate pollution
- Growing "communications overload"

Economic Trends

- development of larger scale, multinational industrial enterprises
- Increasing reliance on theoretical knowledge
- Growth of the service sector
- Continued inflation

Political Trends

- Growing interdependence of nations
- More frequent occurrence of terrorism
- Spread of nuclear weapons
- Increasing egalitarian pressure
- Growing inability of U.S. government to respond rapidly and effectively to problems and crises

Cultural and Social Trends

- Continued predominance of "modernism"
- The rise of the "new class"

---

energy and food, and better techniques for combating pollution. There are some individuals, such as Herman Kahn [11] and, to a certain extent, Daniel Bell [1], who feel that technology can probably meet this challenge. They point out that techniques are likely to be found that will permit the mining of oceans for minerals and food, the use of satellites to spot scarce resources, the control of weather patterns, the exploitation of solar energy, and so on [12]. But even the more optimistic writers recognize that there are certain dangers in relying too heavily on technology to, in a sense, "bail us out" [11]. They all admit that there is a possibility that the needed food sources, energy supplies, and cancer cures (to counteract pollution-caused cancers) will not be found. Moreover, several less optimistic writers have stressed that technological developments often produce dangerous unintended outcomes. For example, the use of nuclear power plants could produce radioactive contamination of the environment [7], and continued development of nuclear and other new methods of generating energy could raise the temperature of the earth's atmosphere to hazardous levels [6, 7, 10]. Likewise, the "green revolution" in agriculture could lead to overplanting of certain "high-yield" strains of grain that would not adapt well to relatively permanent changes in weather conditions (e.g., an end to monsoons) [7].

Concern about resource scarcities, pollution, and potentially dangerous technological developments will motivate many individuals to monitor environmental and technological trends. But such monitoring will become increasingly more difficult because of communications or information "overload" [1, 7]. Society will be bombarded with an even greater volume of information that will be more technical in content and, therefore, more difficult to process. Consequently, a need will arise for larger numbers of reliable translators and processors of information (e.g., independent research and testing agencies) so that the public will be able to keep reasonably well informed.

To produce the technological growth that will be needed to overcome scarcity and pollution problems, it will probably be necessary to erect industrial enterprises that are even larger in scale than today's giant multinational corporations [1, 7]. These organizations will be both publicly and privately owned. However, by erecting mammoth enterprises that will permit the efficient mining of the

191

oceans or the development of nuclear fusion reactors, society will be placing even more and more economic (and political) power in the hands of fewer and fewer people.

Three other significant economic trends should be mentioned. First, there is likely to be more reliance in the future on *theoretical knowledge* to create an economy that will serve the needs of the population [1]. Econometric models will be used more extensively in national economic planning, and management science/operations research models will be used more heavily by individual enterprises. Second, as mentioned previously, the service sector of the economy will grow considerably [1]. There will be a larger proportion of people employed in services, and many of these people will work for private companies involved in providing *public* services. Third, there is likely to be continued inflation for quite some time [1, 2]. Inflation may be the unavoidable result of efforts to keep unemployment low and growth high in an era of scarcity. Clearly, all of these trends could alarm certain individuals. For example, some people might worry that the theories used to manage the economy could be incorrect and likely to produce economic crises, while others might be concerned about the difficulty of trying to improve productivity in the service sector.

The political situations of most nations will be altered significantly as a result of many of the trends identified thus far. Among other things, countries will be increasingly more dependent on one another to obtain scarce resources. While this increased interdependency could lead to a more cooperative spirit among nations, there is also the strong possibility that it would lead to conflicts and crises that would be of a different order of magnitude than the recent "energy crisis," for example. Terrorism—directed at nuclear power plants, for instance—and threats to use nuclear weapons could both become commonplace as resource-poor nations reach points of desperation [7, 10]. In addition, the United States could face considerable, perhaps violent, pressure from egalitarian forces within its own boundaries [1, 5] bent on redistributing wealth from rich people to poor people in all parts of the world. What makes all these political trends particularly unsettling to many people is the growing inability of the U.S. government (and all governments, for that matter) to deal, in a rapid and effective manner, with such problems and crises as terrorism, resource blackmail, and the spread of nuclear weapons [2, 7, 10].

Two trends that should contribute to the rise of anti-industrialism are the continued dominance of "modernism" in the cultural realm [2] and the emergence of a "new class" in the social realm [13]. Modernism, as defined by Bell, should weaken the industrial system and make it easier to attack. As Bell states:

> The characteristic style of industrialism is based on the principles of economics and economizing: on efficiency, least cost, maximization, optimization, and functional rationality. Yet it is this very style that is in conflict with the advanced cultural trends of the Western world, for modernist culture emphasizes anti-cognitive and anti-intellectual modes which look longingly toward a return to instinctual sources of expression. The one emphasizes functional rationality, technocratic decision making, and meritocratic rewards; the other, apocalyptic moods and anti-rational modes of behavior. It is this disjunction which is the historical cultural crisis of all Western bourgeois society. [2, p. 84]

At the same time, the rise of the "new class," as defined by Irving Kristol, should provide a constituency for the anti-industrialism movement. As Kristol states:

> This "new class" consists of scientists, lawyers, city planners, social workers, educators, criminologists, sociologists, public health doctors, etc.—a substantial number of whom find their careers in the expanding public sector rather than the private. The public sector, indeed, is where they prefer to be. They are, as one says, "idealistic"—i.e., far less interested in individual financial rewards than in the corporate power of their class. [13, p. 134]

This class could be said to have become infected by what Robert Heilbroner calls a "civilizational malaise." They are disturbed by "the inability of a civilization directed to material improvement—higher incomes, better diets, miracles of medicine, triumphs of applied physics and chemistry—to satisfy the human spirit" [10, p. 21].

The "new class" and others infected by the "civilizational malaise" are the potential population of the anti-industrialism movement. They will likely attempt to steer society in a direction that would theoretically insure its survival and an improved overall quality of life for all citizens. Whether the anti-industrialists will be motivated by fear, guilt, or, as Amitai Etzioni [8] suggests, self-actualization (the elite "new class" will already have its more basic needs satisfied), is unclear. But one can be fairly certain that they will strive hard to obtain the knowledge, power, and authority they will need to:

- Reduce the wasteful consumption of scarce resources
- Reduce the amount of environmental pollution
- Reduce reliance on technology
- Protect the world from the unintended outcomes of technological development
- Help people deal with communications overload
- Play a significant role in making socially conscious decisions within major industrial enterprises
- Play a significant role in deciding national economic policies
- Improve the public's satisfaction with work roles
- Redistribute much of the wealth of rich people to the poor people of the world
- Eliminate any other serious problems created by industrialism.

SUMMARY AND CONCLUSION

By the year 2000, consumerism as it exists today will probably disappear from the American scene. It will gradually be replaced by a major social movement formed from a convergence of forces that we have chosen to call "anti-industrialism." This new movement will have the support and participation of many of today's consumerists, but it will be concerned with much more basic issues than those addressed by the consumerism movement of the 1960s and 1970s. In fact, the consumerism issues of today will seem trivial when compared to the issues of concern to tomorrow's "anti-industrialists."

We have reached this conclusion after reviewing the printed thoughts of such scholars as Bell, Kahn, Heilbroner, Harman, Ehrlich, Etzioni, and Daly, among others, who have written about the future

194

of what has been labeled "post-industrial society" [1]. These scholars have identified several environmental, technological, economic, political, social, and cultural trends that should clearly transform the nature of consumerism by the year 2000.

In actuality, social forces comparable to an anti-industrialism movement have already emerged [9, 13]. Nevertheless, it will take quite some time before anti-industrialism becomes a major (and perhaps dominant) force in American society. In fact, for the next five to ten years, the consumerism movement—which is not necessarily opposed to present or increased levels of industrialization—is likely to remain an active and influential force that may overshadow any anti-industrialist sentiment. It is predicted, however, that within the next two decades consumerism will become highly institutionalized and individualized. As a result, it is likely that the movement will lose much of its vitality. Furthermore, as problems associated with resource scarcities, pollution, communications overload, and the like become more evident, increasing numbers of people will become more enamored of the anti-industrialism movement and less interested in the relatively minor problems (e.g., bait-and-switch advertising) associated with marketing, unless the latter problems affect them directly and personally.

As with all major social movements, it is likely that major crises will be the primary factors energizing anti-industrialism. Because of the vast number of opportunities for such crises to occur on any one of several fronts (e.g., political, economic, social, technological, cultural, and the like), we feel reasonably certain that the anti-industrialism movement will rise to prominence by the year 2000, if not before. However, no one can foretell whether the movement will be successful in achieving some of its objectives (e.g., conservation of resources, redistribution of wealth). What does seem clear is that such a movement may be necessary if "spaceship earth" is to be guided away from a course that could lead to its ultimate destruction.

REFERENCES

1. Bell, Daniel. *The Coming of Post-Industrial Society.* New York: Basic Books, 1973.

2. _____. *The Cultural Contradictions of Capitalism.* New York: Basic Books, 1976.

3. Bloom, Paul N. "How Will Consumer Education Affect Consumer Behavior," in Beverlee B. Anderson, ed., *Advances in Consumer Research,* Vol. 3, Chicago: Assn. for Consumer Research, 1976, pp. 208-12.

4. Boulding, Kenneth E. "The Economics of the Coming Spaceship Earth," in Henry Jarrett, ed., *Environmental Quality in a Growing Economy.* Baltimore, Md.: Johns Hopkins Press, 1966.

5. Cobbs, John. "Egalitarianism," *Business Week* (Dec. 1, 8, and 15, 1975), 62-65, 86-90, and 86-88, respectively.

6. Daly, Herman E. *Toward a Steady-State Economy.* San Francisco: W. H. Freeman & Co., 1973.

7. Ehrlich, Paul R. and Anne H. Ehrlich. *The End of Affluence.* New York: Ballantine Books, 1974.

8. Etzioni, Amitai. "A Creative Adaption to a World of Rising Shortages," *Annals of the Amer. Academy of Political and Social Sciences,* 420 (July, 1975), 98-109.

9. Harman, W. W. "Notes on the Coming Transformation," in Andrew A. Spekke, ed., *The Next 25 Years: Crisis and Opportunity.* Washington, D.C.: World Future Society, 1975, 10-22.

10. Heilbroner, Robert L. *An Inquiry into the Human Prospect.* New York: W. W. Norton & Co., 1975.

11. Kahn, Herman. "Forces for Change," in Herman Kahn, ed., *The Future of the Corporation.* New York: Mason & Lipscomb Publishers, 1974.

12. _____ and William Brown. "A World Turning Point—And a Better Prospect for the Future," in Andrew A. Spekke, ed., *The Next 25 Years: Crisis and Opportunity.* Washington, D.C.: World Future Society, 1975, 23-42.

196

13. Kristol, Irving. "On Corporate Capitalism in America," *Public Interest,* 41 (Fall 1975), 124-41.

14. "Marketing When the Growth Slows," *Business Week* (Apr. 14, 1975), 45.

15. Schon, Donald A. "Consumerism in Perspective," in Mary G. Jones and David M. Gardiner, eds., *Consumerism: A New Force in Society.* Lexington, Mass.: Lexington Books, 1976.

16. Simmel, Georg. *Conflict.* Glencoe, Ill.: The Free Press, 1955.

17. Wilson, James Q. "The Rise of the Bureaucratic State," *Public Interest,* 41 (Fall 1975), 77-103.

18. Wolfgang, Marvin E., special ed. *Adjusting to Scarcity*, collection of essays appearing in *Annals of the AAPSS,* 420 (July 1975).

PART 6

Consumerism in a Growing Era of Scarcity

THE STEADY-STATE ECONOMY AND
THE CONSUMER

Herman E. Daly
Louisiana State University

*This paper deals with the broad topic of "the steady-state econ-
omy" and its effect on consumers. Daly defines the term* steady-state
*and explains why a steady-state economy is desirable as well as why
this fact has not yet been recognized. Finally, he focuses on the
role of consumers in such an economy.*

INTRODUCTION

For the past several years I have been intrigued by an idea. It is
not at all a new idea. It was expressed in the 1850s by John Stuart
Mill, but has never been taken very seriously by subsequent economists. I think the time to take the idea seriously has now arrived,
and so I take it seriously and have been trying to convince my
fellow economists to do likewise. The idea in question is what Mill
called a "stationary state." I prefer to call it a "steady-state economy." People who don't like the idea tend to call it a "stagnant
economy" or, if they are more fair-minded but still negatively
disposed, a "no-growth" economy. If growth is good, as we have
been told for so long, then no-growth must be bad, so why not
forget it? To avoid such thought-stifling semantic blocks, it is necessary first to define precisely what a steady-state economy is, and
what it is not. Once the concept is well defined, one can ask why
is it an idea whose time has come? Why is a steady-state economy
necessary and/or desirable, and what has kept us from recognizing
this? If the question can be satisfactorily answered, then the next
logical query is: How can a steady-state economy best be achieved?
Can there be a nondisruptive transition from a growth economy
to a steady-state economy? The last is the question that interests
me most right now, but before I can expect others to get very

interested in it, I have to give convincing answers to the first two questions. That is as much as I will attempt in this paper.

One further preliminary point. It is worth remembering that throughout most of his history man has not lived in a growth economy, but rather in something approximating a steady-state economy. Only in the last two hundred years has growth become a dominant feature of economic life. Thus, not only is the idea of a steady-state economy an old one, but so is the corresponding reality. It probably has survival value. A near steady state is the norm. Growth is the aberration.

WHAT IS A STEADY-STATE ECONOMY?

The steady-state economy is defined in *physical* terms. Two physical stocks (or inventories) are held constant: (1) the population of human bodies; and (2) the population of physical artifacts, which may be thought of an extensions of human bodies, if you like. Obviously, people die and artifacts wear out. For the populations to remain constant, there must be births equal to deaths and new production equal to depreciation. Thus, the constancy referred to cannot be a static constancy, but rather it is a dynamic constancy maintained by continuous renewal—in other words, a steady state. The stocks of bodies and artifacts are analogous to lakes that maintain a constant level. But they are not isolated lakes. They are fed by an incoming stream and drained by an outgoing stream. Imput equals output. Input eventually *becomes* output.

Because of the equality and eventual identity of input and output, we can merge the two concepts and call it "throughput." In the case of lakes, the concept of throughput is clear. In the case of populations, the physical mass and organized structure of human bodies is maintained by an inflow of matter-energy to balance the outflow. Not only are whole bodies replaced by births equal to deaths, but the day-to-day maintenance of bodies requires continual replacement of cells. The stock of artifacts likewise requires a continual maintenance flow of matter-energy, both to prevent premature depreciation and to replace worn-out artifacts. In a physical sense, then, the stocks of people and artifacts may be thought of as open systems that maintain their size and their structure in the midst of a continual throughput of matter-energy, just as a lake maintains its size and shape in the midst of a continual throughput of water. The stocks of bodies and artifacts are what yield services and satisfy human wants. The throughput is the cost of maintenance of the stocks of bodies and artifacts. The throughput flow begins with extraction of matter-energy from the natural environment—that is, depletion. There follows a process of production in which the throughput is accumulated and structured into a stock of things that satisfy human wants. The stock exists for a long or short time, yielding its services during the process of consumption. The waste products of consumption and production are sooner or later returned to the natural environment as pollution. The throughput begins with depletion and ends with pollution. Both depletion and pollution are costs; therefore, the throughput is a cost.

What else can we say about throughput? From the first law of thermodynamics we know that matter-energy can neither be created nor destroyed. Production and consumption are really only transformations, because in a physical sense inputs are not "produced," they are taken from the environment, and outputs are not consumed, they are returned to the environment. Moreover, the total amount of matter-energy taken out in depletion must ultimately be returned in the form of pollution. The difference between raw material inputs and waste outputs is qualitative, not quantitative. The matter-energy that comes in is useful matter-energy, that which goes out is useless. In terms of the second law of thermodynamics, inputs are of low entropy, outputs are high entropy. The throughput is the entropic physical flow along which matter-energy is degraded to maintain intact the size and structure of the stocks of people and artifacts. More about entropy later, but for now it was necessary to define throughput, so that in turn we can define steady-state economy.

A steady-state economy is an economy in which the stocks of people and artifacts are held constant at some chosen, desirable level and maintained by the lowest feasible rate of throughput.

Two things should be noted about this definition. First, the level at which stocks are held constant has not been specified, beyond claiming that there is such a thing as a sufficient level. Some amount of people and artifacts has got to be enough. Second, the sufficient stocks should be maintained by low rates of throughput, because throughput is a cost and should be minimized for any chosen level of stocks. The larger the stocks, the larger must be the throughput flow. The shorter lived and less durable the stocks, the larger the throughput flow.

Only two stock magnitudes are constant: the population of human bodies and the inventory of human artifacts. We should emphasize what is *not* held constant. No flow magnitudes are held constant: GNP is not constant, nor is throughput necessarily constant. Technology is not constant, nor is the design or product mix of artifacts constant. The knowledge, goodness, and genetic inheritance of the population are not held constant. The distribution of wealth is not held constant, nor are social and legal institutions. Nothing other than the populations of bodies and artifacts is constant. That leaves much room for change.

If we understand by "growth" a change in *quantity*, and by "development" a change in *quality* or structure, then it is more or less accurate to say that a steady-state economy is a no-growth economy, but it certainly is not a "no-development" economy. By analogy, our planet is a no-growth system, but it certainly experiences qualitative development. The human economy is a subsystem of the planet that has been both growing and developing. It must surely at some point stop growing, but it need not and probably cannot stop developing. Basically, a steady-state economy is a generalization of the demographer's concept of a stationary population to include not only the population of human bodies, but also the extensions of human bodies, in the form of artifacts. Almost everyone admits nowadays that the human population cannot grow forever. Well, neither can the population of cars, houses, airplanes, and power plants. Artifacts, like people, take up space, use up materials and energy, and make depleting and polluting demands on the environment. If one population limit is admitted, how can the other be denied? Why is the notion of a steady-state economy so controversial?

WHY DO WE NEED, AND WANT, A
STEADY-STATE ECONOMY?

Economics has to do with ends and means. The standard, somewhat ponderous, textbook definition of economics is "the study of the allocation of scarce means among competing ends, where the object of the allocation is the maximization of the attainment of those ends"; in other words, how to do the most you can with the little you have.

When economists, and most other people as well, speak of ends and means it is always in the plural. To understand why, consider the entire ends-means spectrum in Figure 1, all the way from the singular ultimate end to the singular ultimate means (our language won't even allow the grammatical singular—we say "a means" rather than "a mean").

The ultimate end is that which is good in and of itself and does not derive its goodness from any instrumental relation to a higher good. It is not a means to anything higher. Philosophers have been trying to pin it down for ages, but they seem recently to have forgotten about it. Intermediate ends exist in a hierarcy. We continually rank and rerank intermediate ends. But with reference to what? With reference to some concept, however vague, of the ultimate end. The very word *priorities* implies not only a ranking but a first place. The ordering of intermediate ends is the task of ethics.

At the other extreme we have ultimate means—that which is useful for satisfying human wants, but is not itself the product or end of any human activity. What is the ultimate useful stuff of our world? It there any common denominator underlying all useful things, something whose supply is given and cannot be increased? The conversion of ultimate means into intermediate means is the job of technology. Economics, in the middle of the spectrum, takes technology and ethics for granted and attempts to find the best allocation of given plural intermediate means supplied by technology among given plural intermediate ends, ranked by ethics.

I believe that the middle position of economics in this spectrum, well isolated from ultimates, has produced a kind of blindness to limits. Intermediate ends seem limitless—who can enumerate them?

205

FIGURE 1
ENDS-MEANS SPECTRUM

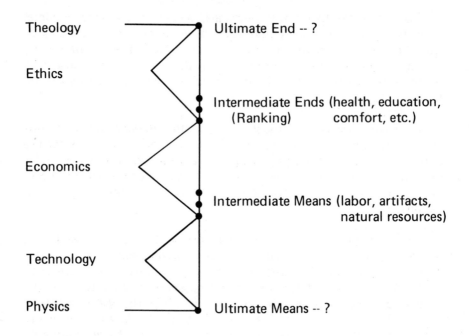

Intermediate means, the products of technology, likewise seem limitless. Economic growth might be defined as the production of ever more intermediate means (artifacts) for the satisfaction of ever more intermediate ends. The economist sees no limit. Some ends may be satiated, but new ones emerge. Some particular resources become depleted, but new substitutes will be found. If we look only at the middle range of the spectrum (the domain of plurality, relativity, and substitutability), it is hard to come to any other conclusion. Our history over the past century lends empirical support to the growth position.

But if we look at the entire ends-means spectrum and especially the extremes, we encounter ultimates: the singular, the absolute, and the limited. Two sets of questions emerge. First, is the nature of the ultimate end such that, beyond some point, it cannot be served by, and in fact may be obstructed by, the further accumulation of stocks of intermediate means? Are all of the ends to which resources are now devoted really worthwhile—could we stop doing certain things and not be any worse off? Second, are there limits to the total supply of ultimate means? Are ultimate means limited in ways that clever technology cannot overcome? I want to suggest that the answer to both sets of questions is *yes*. The nature of the ultimate end, insofar as we can discern it, limits the *desirability* of growth. The nature of ultimate means limits the *possibility* of growth.

Let us first consider the possibility limits imposed by the nature of ultimate means. Thermodynamics teaches us that the ultimate useful means is low-entropy matter-energy. We obtain low entropy from two sources: the flow of solar energy, and the stocks of terrestrial deposits of concentrated minerals. In terms of materials, low entropy means concentration, structure, order. Dispersed, randomly scattered molecules of any material are useless (high entropy). In energy terms, low entropy means the capacity to do work, or concentrated, relatively high-temperature energy. Energy dispersed in equilibrium with the general low-temperature environment is useless (high entropy). The terrestrial mineral source of low entropy is obviously limited in total amount. The solar source is practically unlimited in total amount, but it is strictly limited in its rate of arrival to earth. Both sources of ultimate means are therefore limited—one in total amount, the other in rate of arrival for use.

There is an enormous disproportion in the total amounts of the two sources: If all the earth's fossil fuels could be burned, they would only provide the energy equivalent of a few weeks of sunlight. The sun is expected to shine for another five billion years or so. This raises a cosmically embarrassing economic question: If the solar source is so vastly more abundant, why have we over the last two centuries shifted the physical base of our economy from overwhelming dependence on solar energy and renewable resources, to overwhelming dependence on nonrenewable terrestrial minerals? An important part of the answer, I think, is that terrestrial stocks can, for a while at least, be used up at a rate of man's own choosing—that is, rapidly. Solar energy and renewable resource usage is limited by the fixed solar flux and by the natural rates of growth of plants and animals. This provides a natural constraint on economic growth. Yet growth can be speeded up for a time at least by consuming geological capital—by running down the reserves of terrestrial low entropy. If the object is growth, then it can be achieved most easily by using up terrestrial stocks rapidly. As population and per capita consumption grow beyond the capacity of renewable resources and solar energy to support them, we have all the more need to rely on terrestrial stocks, or geologic capital.

The difficulty is two-fold. First, we will run out of terrestrial sources eventually. Second, even if we never ran out we still would face problems of ecological imbalance caused by a growing throughput of matter-energy. Mankind is the only species that lives beyond the budget of solar income. The whole biosphere has evolved as a complex system around the fixed point of a given solar flux. Now man in escaping the common constraint has gotten badly out of balance with the rest of the biosphere and runs the considerable danger of destroying or at least inhibiting the complex life support systems that all life and wealth depend on. As stocks of people and artifacts have grown, the throughput has had to grow also, implying more depletion and more pollution. Natural biogeochemical cycles become overloaded. Exotic substances are produced and thrown wholesale into the biosphere—substances with which we have had no evolutionary experience and which are consequently nearly always disruptive.

But are we not giving insufficient credit to technology in claiming that ultimate means are limited? Is technology not itself a limitless resource? All technologies, nature's as well as man's, run on an entropy gradient; that is, the total entropy of the outputs of the process must always be greater than the total entropy of inputs. Otherwise we would have a process that violates the second law of thermodynamics, and so far no such process has been observed. Technology uses up low entropy. If low entropy sources are limited, then so is technology. It is ironic to be told by growth boosters that technology is freeing man from dependence on resources. It has done nearly the opposite. It has made us ever more dependent on the scarcer of the two sources of ultimate means. The entropy law tells us that when technology increases order in one part of the universe, it must produce an even greater amount of disorder somewhere else. If that "somewhere else" is the sun (as it is for nature's technology and man's traditional preindustrial technologies), we need not worry. If "somewhere else" is on the earth, then we had

208

better pay attention. The throughput flow maintains or increases the order within the human economy, but it does so at the cost of creating greater disorder in the rest of the natural world, as a result of depletion and pollution. There is a limit to how much disorder can be produced in the rest of the biosphere and still have it function well enough to support the human subsystem.

Although man's technology cannot overcome these limits, it can achieve a better accommodation to them, and can work more in harmony with nature's technology than it has in the past. But this improved accommodation cannot be achieved in a growth context, in an economy that would rather maximize throughput than reduce it. It requires the framework of a steady-state economy.

From these considerations about ultimate means, I conclude that there are limits to the possibility of continued growth and that a steady-state economy will sooner or later become necessary. It is likely to be sooner, when we consider the growing evidence of ecosystem disruption.

Let us turn now to a consideration of the ultimate end and the limits it imposes on the desirability of growth. What is the ultimate end? The fact that one does not know the answer is no excuse for not raising the question, because certainly it is *the* question for all of us. Only a kind of minimum answer to such a maximum question would be likely to command consensus. As a minimum answer, let me suggest that whatever the ultimate end is, it presupposes a respect for, and the survival of, the evolutionary process through which God has bestowed upon us the gift of self-conscious life. Whatever human values are put in first place, their further realization requires the survival of human beings. It may be a noble thing to sacrifice the remaining years of one's own personal life to a higher cause, but to sacrifice the whole evolutionary process to some "higher cause" is surely fanaticism. This minimum answer begs many questions: Survival and evolution of life in what direction? To what extent should the evolutionary process be influenced by man and to what extent should it be left spontaneous? I leave these questions aside. The only point is that survival must rank very high in the ends hierarchy, and consequently any growth that is made possible only by the creation of means that threaten survival should be strictly limited. Is the further growth made possible by the develop-

209

ment of breeder reactors and multi-ton quantities of plutonium really desirable? The distinguished Committee of Inquiry on the Plutonium Economy of the National Council of Churches believes that it is not desirable, and I certainly agree. Others disagree on this specific question. But surely *some* kinds of growth are limited by their undesirability, even though they may be possible. What about growth per se? Are all kinds of physical growth subject to desirability limits? Is there such a thing as "enough" in the material realm, and is enough better than "more than enough"? Certainly all organic needs can be satiated, and to go beyond enough is harmful. The only want that seems insatiable is the want for distinction, the desire to be in some way superior to one's neighbors. The main avenue of distinction in our society is to have a larger income than the next fellow and to spend more. The only way for everyone to earn more is to have aggregate growth. But there is the rub. If everyone earns more then where is the distinction? It is possible for everyone's *absolute* income to increase, but not for everyone's *relative* income to increase. To the extent that it is higher relative income that is important, growth becomes useless. As E. J. Mishan has expressed it:

> In its extreme form—and as affluence rises we draw closer to it—only relative income matters. A man would then prefer a 5% reduction in his own income accompanied by a 10% reduction in the incomes of others, to a 25% increase in both his income and the income of others . . . The more this attitude prevails— and the ethos of our society actively promotes it—the more futile is the objective of economic growth for our society as a whole. For it is obvious that over time everyone cannot become relatively better off. [1]

So even if one's ultimate end is to have more than his neighbor, aggregate growth is limited in its capacity to satisfy that end. It is just like the arms race: If each side achieves the capacity to annihilate the other side 20 times over instead of only 10 times over, nothing has really changed, except that a lot more resources have been wasted.

From the not very original premises that survival is good and that enough is as good as, or better than, more than enough, I conclude that growth beyond some point becomes undesirable, even if still possible. Therefore, a steady-state economy becomes desirable.

What can we say about *when* a steady-state economy becomes desirable?

We do not satisfy ends in any random order. We satisfy our most pressing needs first. We do not use resources in any random order. We use the highest grade and most accessible resources first. This elementary rule of sensible behavior underlies the law of dinimishing marginal benefit and the law of increasing marginal cost. As growth continues, at some point the curve of falling marginal benefits of growth will intersect the curve of rising marginal costs. At that point growth should cease. Economists would not deny the logic, but they would rightly object that the analysis is too static. Technology shifts the whole cost curve downward. New wants can push the whole benefits curve upward. Looked at statically, the curves have opposite slopes and will certainly intersect. But considered dynamically, technical and psychological change will push the curves apart so fast that their intersection will forever remain far ahead of us. That is the faith of the growth economist.

Our consideration of ultimate means and ultimate ends has raised insuperable problems for the growth economist. Technology is limited in its ability to lower costs. Technology uses up ultimate means and cannot create them. New wants in affluent societies tend to be relative wants of distinction, and aggregate growth cannot make everyone relatively better off. Ultimate means limit the downward shift of the cost curve. The nature of the ultimate end limits the upward shift of the benfits curve.

I think the case for the necessity and desirability of the steady-state economy must be admitted. But we have not said when. Maybe it won't be necessary for another thousand years. Maybe we can grow for a long time yet. Maybe we have not yet reached the optimum size.

Even if we have not yet reached the optimum size, we should still learn to live in a steady-state economy so that we can remain at the optimum once we get there, rather than grow through it. If we achieve a steady-state economy at one level, we are not forever frozen at that level. If we later discover that a larger of smaller stock would be better, we can either grow or decline to the preferred level, at which we would again be stable. (Growth or decline would then be a temporary adjustment process, and not a norm.) I believe, however, that we have passed the optimum and will in the future probably have to reduce population and per capita consumption. But the issue of optimum level is very difficult to handle, because a number of related questions must be answered simultaneously: (1) What size population do we want, (2) living at what level of per capita resource consumption, (3) for how long, and (4) on the basis of what kinds of technology? Also, we must ask whether the level we choose for the U.S. should be generalizable to the world as a whole. With 6 percent of the world's population, we, in the U.S. now consume about 30 percent of the world's annual production of nonrenewable resources. To generalize the U.S. standard of per capita consumption to the entire world requires a six-fold increase in current resource throughput. In addition, to supply the rest of the world with the average per capita "standing crop" of industrial metals already embodied in the existing artifacts in the ten richest nations, would require more than 60 years' world production of these metals at 1970 rates [2]. The ecological disruption caused by the next six-fold increase will be much greater per unit or resource produced because of diminishing returns. Even technological optimists like Dr. Alvin Weinberg recognize the heat limit to energy use:

> Man was increasing his production of energy by about 5% per year: within 200 years at this rate he would be producing as much energy as he receives from the sun. Obviously, long before that time man would have to come to terms with global climatological limits imposed on his production of energy. Although it is difficult to estimate just how soon we shall have to adjust the world's energy policies to take this limit into account, it might well be as little as 30 to 50 years. [3]

These considerations make me doubt very strongly that present U.S. levels of living are generalizable, either to the world as a whole or to very many future generations. Attempts at such generalization are likely to embrace unacceptable technologies. So I think the sooner we move to a steady-state economy, the better.

A steady-state economy is not a panacea. Even it will not last forever; nor will it overcome diminishing returns. But it will permit our economy to die gracefully of old age rather than prematurely from the cancer of growthmania.

THE CONSUMER IN THE STEADY-STATE ECONOMY

What can we say about the role of the consumer in a steady-state economy? I would like for you to answer that question rather than me, but to break the ice I will briefly list a few thoughts. First, perhaps we should quit calling ourselves "consumers" and start calling ourselves "conservers," or at least "conserving users." The steady-state economy is a *conserver society*, not a *consumer society*. There must be a large shift of emphasis from production to maintenance. Marketing techniques must become less sales oriented and more service oriented. Perhaps rental of artifacts with maintenance contracts will become more common for those goods whose maintenance is difficult or requires high technology. Durability and life expectancy of artifacts will be more important, as will be efficiency in the sense of increasing the load factor on artifact use. Nieghborhood tool rental and maintenance centers can reduce the excess population of idle lawnmowers, edgers, trimmers, power drills, saws, and so on, that are badly maintained and lying mostly idle in garages.

The average conserver will spend less time shopping for new items and more time servicing and acquiring the maintenance skills to make what he has last longer. More people will be employed in maintenance, fewer in production.

Of course, recycling will become vastly more important, and artifacts will be designed for ease of recyclability and repair. Marketing of scrap and all sorts of waste will become important. Instead of a throw-away mentality, the motto will be "use it up, make it last, repair it, wear it out, and then recycle what is left."

As people become more conservers and less consumers, they will acquire a greater degree of independence and autonomy. For example, as one learns to conserve his own body and health, he becomes less a consumer of medicine and doctor's services, and less

213

at the mercy of the AMA (the *other* AMA). Increased conservation of artifacts makes us less dependent on the producers who are so anxious to replace these items as rapidly as possible.

REFERENCES

1. Mishan, E. J. "Growth and Anti-Growth: What Are the Issues?," *Challenge*, May/June 1973.

2. Brown, Harrison. "Human Materials Production as a Process in the Biosphere," *Scientific American,* 223 (Sept. 1970), pp. 194-208.

3. *Science*, 186 (Oct. 18, 1974).